Something Absolute

Surviving a Miracle

First published by O Books, 2009
O Books is an imprint of John Hunt Publishing Ltd., The Bothy, Deershot Lodge, Park Lane, Ropley,
Hants, SO24 0BE, UK
office1@o-books.net
www.o-books.net

Distribution in:

UK and Europe
Orca Book Services
orders@orcabookservices.co.uk
Tel: 01202 665432 Fax: 01202 666219
Int. code (44)

USA and Canada
NBN
custserv@nbnbooks.com
Tel: 1 800 462 6420 Fax: 1 800 338 4550

Australia and New Zealand
Brumby Books
sales@brumbybooks.com.au
Tel: 61 3 9761 5535 Fax: 61 3 9761 7095

Far East (offices in Singapore, Thailand,
Hong Kong, Taiwan)
Pansing Distribution Pte Ltd
kemal@pansing.com
Tel: 65 6319 9939 Fax: 65 6462 5761

South Africa
Alternative Books
altbook@peterhyde.co.za
Tel: 021 555 4027 Fax: 021 447 1430

Text copyright Ruth Jolly 2008

Design: Stuart Davies

ISBN: 978 1 84694 235 8

A CIP catalogue record for this book is available
from the British Library.

Printed by Digital Book Print

O Books operates a distinctive and ethical publishing philosophy in
all areas of its business, from its global network of authors to
production and worldwide distribution.
This book is produced on FSC certified stock, within ISO14001
standards. The printer plants sufficient trees each year through
the Woodland Trust to absorb the level of emitted carbon in
its production.

Something Absolute

Surviving a Miracle

Ruth Jolly

BOOKS

Winchester, UK
Washington, USA

Acknowledgements

Simone Weil in Assisi by Edward Hirsch is part of a longer poem: *Away from Dogma* in the collection, *Earthly Measures* Edward Hirsch, Published Alfred A Knopf New York 2003.

Paul Avis (Ed) *The Resurrection of Jesus Christ* Darton Longman & Todd 1993

Louis de Bernieres *Captain Corelli's Mandolin* Martin Secker & Warburg 1994

Marshall I.H. *The Acts of the Apostles: An Introduction and Commentary.* Inter-Varsity Press 2000

The New English Bible (Collins) is the translation used throughout this book, with occasional quotations from the *Authorised Version*.

CONTENTS

She disliked the miracles in the gospels.
She never believed in the mystery of contact
here below, between a human being and God
She despised popular tales of apparitions.

But that afternoon in Assisi she wandered
through the ... Santa Maria degli Angeli
and happened upon a little marvel of Romanesque
purity where St. Francis liked to pray.

She was there a short time when something absolute
and omnivorous, something she neither believed
nor disbelieved, something she understood ...
... forced her to her knees.

From Simone Weil in Assisi

By Edward Hirsch

CONFUSION

Until Charlie's miracle I took springtime for granted. To be sure, on a crisp February morning I'd enjoy seeing the first snowdrops and watching a pale sun melt the early- morning frost in our city garden, but I can't say I was moved with a deep sense of gratitude or wonder. It was simply spring. The emergence of new life happened, with or without my noticing, year upon year – and mostly it occurred largely unnoticed by me. Until the miracle, that is.

On a cold February day – his 23rd birthday – my younger son Charlie crashed in a light aircraft. He'd just begun training for a Private Pilot's Licence. It was a foul day but he was keen, and his flying instructor took him up in spite of the weather. In the event, circuits and bumps proved impossible in the high wind so they landed at Turweston, a small airfield in north Buckinghamshire, drank a cup of coffee and discussed what to do next. It was clear Charlie would get no more practice that day but his young, sympathetic instructor decided he could at least demonstrate to him the procedure for a recovery from engine failure after take-off. That accomplished, they'd head back to base at Oxford airport.

From the aircraft's tiny cockpit the instructor radioed his intentions to the control tower. They took off. He throttled back the engine. The Cessna hung in the air for a second, its take-off and landing flaps unaccountably in the wrong position. Then it dived into the ground. The instructor was killed instantly; Charlie, on the side that impacted first, lived.

How? No-one can say for sure. Certainly no one who witnessed the crash expected him to. And even after he was airlifted to hospital and rushed to theatre and hooked up to a host of machines in Intensive Care, no one could say whether he'd live or die. But he lived. And as he was moved from one hospital to another for reconstructive and plastic surgery, spring came.

As Charlie's hold on consciousness became gradually stronger, shoots and buds and tiny new leaves appeared. Along the Woodstock Road in Oxford, my daily route to hospital, first one, then another, then masses of pink-blossomed trees burst into exuberant flower. Spring. Life. Hope. A new beginning.

So spring, for me, is all part of the miracle. And this February – as every year now – I'm waiting for spring to rekindle those familiar feelings of optimistic expectation.

January has been unseasonably warm and some of the earliest white blossom in the city has been just a whisker away from bursting forth ... but then ... last week the wind swung round to the north-east and suddenly now there is bitter cold. Spring has been stopped in its tracks. For days, sleet, borne on these freezing winds has made it simply too cold to be comfortable outside. The miracle I was waiting to re-live has been postponed, and suddenly, I'm right back in those agonising first days and weeks after the crash. The bleakness of a winter I shudder to remember, despite its miracle.

A miracle is an enigma. What it's *not*, is a 'happy ending' to a parlous tale; anybody who's been through one will tell you that. A miracle strikes like a bolt of lightning from a thunder cloud. It turns lives inside out and upside down. A miracle is a watershed experience.

*

When I was six I was chosen to act a very small part in a Sunday-school play. Most of the other children were older and had speaking roles. Me? I just had to act surprised ... which I did with every fibre of my small being. I was Jairus' daughter's mother and during the two performances of the play I felt real sorrow as I knelt beside my little daughter, dead on her pallet. I felt hope as the boy playing Jesus came close to our house and then entered. And I felt astonishment and gladness as he raised her from the dead. Then he and his entourage left our corner of the stage and went off to another scene, elsewhere. And I felt satisfaction and pride as my teacher helped me off the stage, praising my contribution – but I also couldn't help feeling a kind of emptiness as the drama rolled on without me.

I never forgot this short experience, and when I had children of my own, I often idly wondered how on earth Jairus' daughter's mother coped with life *after* the miracle. How did she ever manage to get excited about the price of fish again?

For when something truly extraordinary happens to you, the minutiae of life by which your days are shaped and your energy is expended, cease to matter. Yet you must live. In the market place, in the house, at the computer screen, on the telephone, you must get it together. But how? And given that you've clearly enjoyed the greatest of good fortune, will anybody notice you're struggling?

For a long time – a very long time – after a miracle, you flounder, and in a way, there are no more certainties ever again. Something has happened for which there is no clear, solid explanation. And try as you might to re-order events in a logical, factual way, at the heart of it all there remains a mystery. One simply has to cobble together some words that sound vaguely plausible and leave it at that.

No, a miracle, wondrous though it is, is not 'a happy ending'. Rather it is a shattering new beginning, and when the world starts to turn again, what you make of it is seriously down to you.

*

Of course, Charlie's miracle was rather an everyday sort of miracle. On a scale of 1 – 10 I don't suppose it would rate more than a 2. Every medical doctor has a story to tell about the patient who inexplicably survived and prospered against all the odds. And actually, I don't think miracles are all that uncommon. Most of us will come across at least one during our lifetime.

But, then, what *is* a miracle? Speaking personally, let me say straight away I can't cope with the idea of 'divine favours,' and I struggle to see the need for things 'supernatural'. To my mind, whatever exists – including God, however we frame our concept of this unverifiable notion of the transcendent – must be absolutely part and parcel of the natural order of things. So, returning to 'what is a miracle?' I'd say it simply is an unforeseen but joyous event that occurs despite all known probabilities that it wouldn't, shouldn't or couldn't happen. Of course, it isn't simple in practice, but looking at life in general, I think miracles do happen all the time.

We're very uncomfortable with them, though. Our modern minds crave exact explanations for unexpected phenomena. We insist that if an event is not measurable and is experimentally unrepeatable it is only puzzling because pieces of the jigsaw are missing. If we knew more facts, all would be clear. Wouldn't it? Me, I'm not sure that it would. There comes a point in many cases where we have to say that the normal rules by which we antic- ipate cause and effect just don't seem to have operated; something quite random seems to have occurred. The result? Call it fortunate coincidence if you want, but if, like me, you lay claim to a rather vague, private but precious, religious faith, you're stuck with the worrying possibility that you might have at least to consider the word 'miracle'. And having, for myself, rejected the idea of divine intervention I admit it bothers me no end that I cannot get my head around the mystery of Charlie's own workaday miracle. But I have to accept there is no definitive, objective explanation for his survival and recovery and I'll inevitably continue to puzzle over it.

Dead end? Well, no, because what I *can* or should be able to get my head around is the business of what happened next. *After* the miracle. To put myself 'for real' in the position of Jairus' daughter's mother. Now that I have some distance in time, I think I could do that - and perhaps learn something. For it seems to me that the consequences of Charlie's small miracle have run an intriguing, volatile and in large part, unexpected, course.

*

So, this freezing Lenten February as I wait for spring to be re-scheduled, I gaze at the rows of theology books in the city library. Charlie's miracle has had that effect on me: reading theology, I mean. Because, if I'm truthful, before all this happened I'd actually stopped wrestling with questions of religion. In typical middle-aged fashion, I guess I thought I'd reached all the religious conclusions I was going to, and was comfortable with a faith I called 'liberal Christian' but was disinclined to probe. The accident's changed all that, for faced with Charlie's miracle, I've found myself increasingly compelled to re-think my under-standing of what it *means* to be Christian.

It's not a comfortable exercise; it's an ongoing, doubt-and-diffi-culty plagued endeavour - in Lent especially. I say this because for the last few years I've tried at this time to ponder a piece of spiritual writing in a 'read and reflect' *Lectio Divina* fashion.

Lectio Divina? Yes, well, before I actually tried it, I thought *Lectio* was a 'minority sport' practised only by monks and the extremely devout. Therefore definitely not for me. But, hearing about it every now and again, it didn't seem all that difficult, and it occurred to me that this way of approaching a text was pretty much like reading a poem, and I can do that.

At its simplest - bearing in mind I'm at the bottom end of the learning curve - *Lectio* involves reading a short piece through, preferably aloud, with an open mind. Then, if or when something about it resonates, reading it again, this time slowly and carefully for meaning, considering what the writer aimed to convey. Historical context, literary allusions, biographical considerations and so forth – any or all of these might shed light on the studying bit of the process. But just when you've formed some conclusions, the most interesting part begins. You put it down. Maybe leave it for a day or so, or perhaps if you're on a roll, get up and make a cup of tea. Whereupon, you return to the piece to ask: 'How does this speak *to me*? Why does it intrigue/ irritate/ move me? What thoughts does it set in train? And how does it deepen my understanding of life?' I guess I should quote a monastic 'expert' on its value:

Lectio Divina is not only a means of discovering something about God; it also helps us to understand our hidden selves. It is not the alienating absorption of a message that is foreign or even hostile to our deepest aspirations; it is the surprising conclusion that our most authentic level of being is mirrored in the scriptures. (Fr Michael Casey)

I understand the experienced practitioner moves through reading, meditation, prayer and contemplation – but I haven't really got to be that systematic yet. Nevertheless, I use the six weeks of Lent to have a go.

So, having decided to try and take hold of Charlie's miracle this Lent, I'm at the city library to invest in some relevant reading and hopefully, to decide on a text. I start to look for something with 'miracle' in the title but before I know it, my eye is caught by a slim paperback called *The Resurrection*. Resurrection! The absolute number 10 on the inexplicable scale! I shy away from it, not being up for defining my faith too tightly ...

As a member of a congregation I turn up on a Sunday fairly regularly, but I'm not amongst the inner circle of church activists and I feel uncomfortable with Christians who seem to have no problems with their faith. I don't attend a house group or a study circle – and I'd half like to, but I'm so put off by fervent convictions and intellectual dogmatism, I don't dare.

The way into religion for me is through awe and mystery, I know that, but I do realise I have to think as well. Trouble is, the churches don't seem to cater for people like me in whom spiritual conviction co-exists with intellectual ambivalence. I'm no theologian (apart from an ancient A-level in RE, academically I'm History and the Social Sciences) but as a rank-and-file worshipper, I yearn for confirmation that hardly anyone finds the issue of 'belief' easy. Anyway, I read; steadily but unsystematically, and if I'm honest, with a tendency to seek affirmation for my own spiritual outlook. I'd probably do better in some kind of group but, lacking one, I plough on quietly, trying to use Lent as a period for more disciplined reflection than usual.

But, no, surely I can't start with *The Resurrection?* I mean, if I can't get to grips with Charlie's grade 2 miracle, I haven't the slightest chance of sorting out Easter. Well, not the mystery of the Resurrection itself. Nevertheless, I seem to have picked up the book. It's quite new, in good condition. I like that. It has contributions from a number of authors, each coming from a different angle. I like that too. I move down the shelving but keep the paperback in my hand, intending to replace it when I find something more obviously helpful.

A fat paperback commentary on *Acts* sits squashed between books about the gospels and material on St Paul and the epistles. This isn't what I'm looking for either, yet I pause for thought. Not since the aforementioned A-levels have I read through *Acts* (and that's a seriously long time ago) but it's a biblical book I really like … and it occurs to me that, as with Charlie's miracle, I could maybe look at *consequences*. Resurrection appearances in the gospels raise all manner of questions for me and I'd have to start with these – but *Acts* seems simpler. And if I want to think about how people survive a miracle, could I choose a better example than the story of the first Christians? Not, of course, that their 'storm force 10' miracle is in the same league as Charlie's, but it strikes me I might learn something.

I prise the volume off the shelf and glance at the early chapters. *Acts* starts as a mish- mash. One event tumbling after another with little apparent connection and no real attempt to make sense of things. And it hits me between the eyes. How similar it is to the scruffy little diary I kept sporadically after Charlie's crash! A jumble of facts, dates, impressions, hopes and fears. Everything that happened, or seemed to happen, in the aftermath of our own small miracle. Well, obviously, *Acts* has vastly more literary merit, but what I recognise straight away is that urgent, unsettling sense of improvisation. The apostles not sitting down to strategically plan their lives, but life somehow taking hold of them and sweeping them along. Yes, that's how it was. Exhilarating, scary, confusing, exhausting. It rings absolutely true.

I have my text: in fact, I have two.

*

4th Feb. Approx. 12.15 aircraft crashed. Fire crew with cutting gear from Brackley. Airlift to John Radcliffe Hospital, Oxford.

Major injuries: R lung punctured and collapsed at scene, L lung collapsed on admission. Multiple rib fractures, L & R arms fractured, jaw fracture, R leg very severely damaged. Surgery to drain chest and stabilise L arm and R leg.

That's all I wrote – about a week later. In fact, at the start, I had no intention of keeping diary; all I was doing was recording the most basic of facts. The events of that day I will never forget anyway. If people ask me, I can describe them in minute detail. The same goes for other members of the family, so together, our accounts should make a coherent whole. Only they never quite do.

I was the last one to know. At the time of the crash I was

enjoying a light lunch with my mother in the Galeries Lafayette in Paris. Though February is not perhaps the obvious month to take an elderly lady on a four day trip to Paris, it was her birthday (the same day as Charlie's) and she'd never visited the city. I'd had a wonderful time showing her the sights and after our final lunch we made our way back to our small hotel off the Champs Elysees. A freezing wind buffeted us to the Gare du Nord (did we go by taxi or take the Metro? I forget now) and we were happy to settle into the comfortable seats of the London-bound Eurostar. En route, we drank a birthday glass of champagne and looked forward to the evening back at home. Did I experience any premonition of trouble? Any forebodings? None. Leaving the train at Waterloo I did hope that everything was all right at home, as you do, but then another train had to be caught – and it was much too cold to hang around. Had I known just how far from 'all right' home was ... but I didn't. I'd no mobile phone then, and anyway, there was no faster way of getting back, even had I known.

9.30pm, and helping my mother out of the taxi, I noticed by the light of a street lamp there was something odd about the cars outside our house. Later I realised the oddity was that Charlie's dilapidated old banger was missing. But I had no chance to ponder this, since as soon as I lifted my key to the front door it was opened by husband Peter, who quite expressionlessly said: "Come upstairs."

I climbed the stairs to the first floor sitting room, my head confused and my heart beating fast, but nothing prepared me for what came next. Motioning me to sit down, Peter said quietly: "Charlie's aeroplane crashed."

I heard myself cry out in shock. A strange, anguished animal cry and I put my head in my hands.

"They've taken him to the JR."

"Is he going to die?" I demanded, looking up.

"No!" Peter responded defiantly.

Though I realised he couldn't know this, I also understood that Charlie was at least alive as we spoke. Then I wept.

Daughter Sarah and elder son Tim had been waiting downstairs and now they came in.

We clung to one another for comfort. How terrible it had been for them. First to be summoned home – Sarah from Edinburgh, Tim from London – not knowing whether their brother would still be alive when they arrived. Then waiting for me to return from Paris, dreading having to tell me.

Tim had been the first to arrive and had met his father at the John Radcliffe Hospital – in one of those ominous side-rooms where relatives are put who need privacy. They were told that Charlie had been intermittently conscious as they'd brought him in, he'd yelled a bit and sworn … which was encouraging. They'd rushed him into theatre. The Trauma Consultant was unable to give any firm prognosis but said that Charlie clearly had serious chest problems. Turning from these, he added they might also have to amputate his right leg. He was calm and kind, not holding out false hopes but concentrating on facts. He advised Peter and Tim to go home. The hospital would telephone, he promised, as soon as there was any news. It would be some hours.

At home, Peter took a phone call from Charlie's good friend, his schooldays girlfriend Melissa, cheerfully ringing from a job in Italy to wish him a happy birthday. Peter explained the situation as calmly as he could under the circumstances but there was no disguising its gravity. A long way from home, shaken and unable to help, it was a ghastly thing for her to hear. Peter was worried for her but she reassured him she was OK and would ring home. Then daughter Sarah, after a nightmare flight from Scotland, arrived tearstained and bedraggled … and still there was no news and still they had to wait for me.

I listened as they told me all this and felt sick at not being there. My mother was stunned. It was their birthday. Hers and Charlie's. Birthdays weren't meant to be like this. My sister arrived and put her arm around Mum; she'd take her home. As they were gathering up her things, the phone rang. Peter was there like a shot. The message was short. Charlie was out of theatre and in Intensive Care. We could go up to the hospital as soon as we liked.

Towards midnight, Peter, Sarah, Tim and I entered the brightly-lit unit. It was not like other hospital wards. The beds weren't neatly placed against the walls but almost higgledy-piggledy, each one surrounded by an array of medical machinery. There was a buzz of purposeful activity, plenty of nurses and equipment that bleeped and blinked and drew lines. The patients were all unconscious. This I expected ... but *that* patient, over there, was my son. As I quickened my pace towards him I could see he looked terrible, but much more importantly, I could *feel* he was alive. It was extraordinary; though hooked up to a battery of machines, he nevertheless radiated a force – a life force – I could feel before I got to him. It was tangible.

A moment later and I was at his side, stroking his forehead. Wonderful. His broken jaw was swollen, distorting his face and his deep brown eyes were closed. But he lived. Steeling ourselves, however, we asked our questions. Brain damage? Impossible to say, but they were hopeful. Paralysis? Impossible to say but again, they were hopeful. They were pleased with the way in which he'd come through surgery; he was strong. They were not so optimistic about his right leg, although they hadn't amputated since he still had a knee and an ankle joint. If his general condition allowed it, if he continued to hold his own, they would think about the limb next. In the meantime, a ventilator breathed for Charlie and he was deeply sedated. Leaving him that night was agony for all of us.

*

That's the way it is, isn't it? Prompted by 3 or 4 lines of the scruffy diary the memories come tumbling out until it takes quite an effort to stop. Panic! This is a crazy idea! The diary is impossibly painful to read. And what use is it? Yes, it contains facts ... but when it comes to interpretation, it's not even remotely objective.

What I'm getting at, is that nobody this close to a miracle needs to write it down lest they forget. Every detail of my experience remains etched on my brain indelibly. It's only later, when other people ask, that things may thoughtfully get written down. And if they do, the written narrative is bound to be partial, and biased. Much will depend on who tells the story, and for whom. I'm well aware that my account of Charlie's survival would differ markedly in detail and emphasis from Peter's or Sarah's or Tim's – and we were all there, together. And as time has gone by, like ripples in a pond, the effects of Charlie's miracle have touched wider circles of people. And now there are not one but several stories - all of them 'true', probably none of them 'accurate'. And that's just Charlie.

*

So, calming down and skimming a few chapters of my background *Resurrection* book (which I did after all take out of the library) I find I don't have any problem with the *variety* of the Resurrection stories. I'm comfortable with the thought that all of them grasp an element of the truth whilst none is necessarily 'accurate'. For the gospel accounts are far from unanimous about what actually took place, its chronology or the 'eye- witnesses' around whom the narratives are woven. I confess this used to bother me, but now I've relinquished the concept of scripture as some kind of holy journalism, I discover the power and the truth of those stories in which history and legend are inextricably mixed; texts whose facts are unverifiable but whose essential veracity is displayed in their impact.

Whatever it was that happened around Jesus, it clearly stunned and staggered his disciples, so that attempts at explanation were a long time coming. And though from the gospels the general direction of the narrative emerges forcefully, its component parts seem to originate from different times and different sources and one has to admit that the whole is quite hopelessly confused.

I have at least to look at it, the miracle of the Resurrection, and with sinking heart I know I shall have plenty of questions but few answers. But if I'm to consider the aftermath of the miracle, I need briefly to postpone my slow-reading of *Acts* and begin with the confused astonishment of the event itself.

To start with consensus. I suppose if they agree on little else, all four evangelists record that Jesus died on a Roman cross in Jerusalem. They agree that he died, not gloriously, but the agonising, humiliating death of a condemned criminal. And they're united in their insistence that the crucified Jesus did indeed die. But then what happened? Was there darkness? An earthquake? John fails to mention it. Did one of the soldiers pierce Jesus' side? The synoptics don't say so. The evangelists agree that Joseph of Arimathea obtained Pilate's permission to remove the body; that he placed it in a rock tomb and that the entrance was sealed with a stone. It was left, all four relate, during the observation of the Jewish Sabbath. Was it guarded? Matthew is at pains to insist it was.

So who came to the tomb early on the Sunday morning? Women, yes. But was it Mary Magdelene, Mary the mother of James, and Salome as Mark describes – or just the two Marys, as Matthew says? Luke makes no mention of Salome but includes instead Joanna, while John has Mary Magdalene going to the garden alone. And what did they see? That the stone had been rolled away and the body of Jesus was missing. In Mark's account a youth in a white robe told the women that Jesus had been raised and directed them to let the disciples and Peter know he was going before them into Galilee. Whereupon, he added, the women fled in terror saying nothing to anybody. Matthew's two Marys were addressed in much the same terms, though not by a youth but an angel. And instead of running away, the women went immediately to tell the disciples what had occurred. In Luke, the women saw two men in dazzling garments who told them Jesus had risen, and they were terrified, but they went and told the disciples – who didn't believe them.

John relates the fullest and most moving story of the morning's events but a version that differs markedly from the others. Mary Magdalene, on seeing the stone had been rolled away and the body was missing, ran to Simon Peter and the disciple whom Jesus loved. They returned with her and saw for themselves – but no angel, no message. And after they'd gone home, Mary, lingering, turned and met Jesus himself. 'Thinking him to be the gardener ...' that particular story always sends shivers down my spine.

But what to make of all this? The essential miracle of the Christian experience and no one even seems to know who was actually there to bear witness to it...

*

Six o'clock and I woke from a fitful doze with heart pounding. Peter, sleeping lightly beside me, sensed at once that I was awake. The telephone on our bedside table had been mercifully silent all night, though this had not, in itself, allowed us much sleep. Nevertheless, we had hope. I felt physically sick as I thought of the hopeless ordeal Charlie's flying instructor's parents would be going through. It was too much. I couldn't stay with such pain. I had to focus on hope. How early could we ring Intensive Care? Now? Cup of tea first, was Peter's suggestion. He staggered blearily downstairs and reappeared with a couple of mugs – it was still only ten past six. Wait a bit. They'd absolutely promised they'd contact us if Charlie deteriorated and we'd heard nothing. The tea was hot and soothing but I was barely half-way through it before I simply had to phone.

The nurse on the line kindly brushed aside my stumbling apologies for ringing so early. Charlie, she said, had had a reasonably good night and we could come in whenever we wanted. Such relief! Shouted enquiries from Sarah and Tim demonstrated that they, too, were awake and aware I was talking to the hospital.

We made much of the positive news. Not only was Charlie still alive, he'd had 'a reasonably good night'! So tense had we all been, attempting to sleep, we laughed aloud with relief and couldn't stop... manic, defiant laughter as we washed and dressed in haste. Then breakfast. Common sense dictated we should eat something before we left, so we made a plate of toast, but it tasted like cardboard and all we could manage was another mug of tea. We were at the hospital absurdly early. There was really nowhere else to be.

*

Ignorant and credulous they weren't. Well, I don't think so. They knew perfectly well that Jesus was dead. Dead and buried. No wonder they didn't believe the women. And it wasn't at all like a healing. Not like Jairus' daughter. In the Old and the New Testaments there are stories of people presumed dead, restored to life – but they were restored to resume their earthly existence. This thing that had begun to happen around Jesus was of a completely different order. For Jesus seemed to have quietly returned to his friends. Not as he had been in the past – quite frequently they failed to recognise him - but he wasn't insubstantial. He would speak, console them and sometimes he even seemed to eat and drink with them, though not for very long. After a while he would disappear from their sight.

What was happening? Were they mad? Had grief and shame made them vulnerable to the weirdest suggestions? A highly likely explanation, and one I'd definitely go with, but for the fact that stress-generated off-the-wall weirdness doesn't tend to last. This did. It seems that, inconveniently, inexplicably, the disciples began once again to perceive a solid presence of Jesus amongst them. A presence that was altered but not extinguished by his physical death.

*

Beds in Intensive Care are very high from the ground, so that patients who need constant attendance and monitoring can be cared for without too much bending. The patients are not about to get out of bed anyway. That second day I sat for hours on a high stool, on the left side of Charlie's bed, stroking his hair and gently talking to him. Every now and again a doctor or nurse would approach, explain to Charlie what they were going to do, and then examine him. Charlie would occasionally respond with a movement or a sound – he wasn't kept permanently under the deepest sedation – and although this didn't signify a great deal, his reactions nevertheless seemed positive and appropriate. From time to time the nurses would encourage us to leave his side, to have a walk and get something to eat and drink. I found it an almost impossible request. Not that I was doing anything medically useful, sitting with Charlie, except I felt I *was*.

Off-the-wall weirdness again, but that 'life force' I'd sensed in Charlie the moment I'd entered the unit, I now felt strongly in myself and in every person who came to his bedside. It was, I don't know – something *elemental* and I felt that all of us were enfolding Charlie and giving something of our own vital energy to him. It was a purposeful thing I was engaged in, and though I couldn't (and didn't) explain, I was totally engrossed. Meal times came and went and I think I had to be gently persuaded by my son, daughter or husband to take an occasional break. Even then, everywhere in the hospital I felt life. It was like the constant throbbing of the engines on a cross-channel ferry.

*

In the empty tomb part of the Easter narrative, the focus suddenly comes to rest on women. Women making their early-morning way to the tomb to lament and embalm, only to discover that the body of Jesus was missing. Judaism, being rooted in a strongly patriarchal culture, doesn't feature many stories of females. Christianity doesn't do a great deal better for heroines, but quite a lot of women actually appear in the gospels, albeit fleetingly. And two, of course, are in a league of their own: Mary the mother of Jesus and Mary Magdalene. Archetypal figures, both of them.

Being brought up a Protestant, it was years before I began to appreciate that there was much of a female dimension at all in Christianity. And even when I'd started to grasp the spiritual importance of these two women named Mary, my interest was purely objective.

But suddenly that winter's day, I was entirely and only a mother at the bedside of her critically ill son, waiting and hoping. Suddenly and seriously I was living the archetype. I was Woman and if I let myself think, I instinctively knew what the core of that meant: womb and tomb, pain and joy, giving birth, easing death, generation and regeneration, sensuality and wisdom, constancy and compassion.

Mary the mother with her infant. Mary the anxious parent of the lost boy. Mary of the pieta, cradling her crucified son. Mary, the sensual woman with the long hair, with patience to sit at the feet of the teacher and wisdom to understand that the essence of life is extravagant, self-giving generosity. Mary: the archetypal Marys, who no matter what, are there to the end – and beyond the end to a beginning.

Me. At that time and in that place.

*

Arriving home that evening, there was a casserole and a card on the doorstep. More cards on the mat as we pushed open the front door. Seeing our return, neighbours arrived with arms full of flowers delivered into their safekeeping during the day. Hugs and garbled updates as we were surrounded by anxious faces, people unsure what to say to us and uneasy lest our news was not good. But Charlie was still alive, his condition had not deteriorated and today the medics had talked in general terms about tomorrow.

Indoors, the telephone answer-machine blinked, its tape filled to capacity with messages; it was all quite overwhelming. So we laid the dining table, opened a bottle of wine and ate the casserole. It was the first time I remember actually *tasting* anything since the accident and it was very good. Flowers and cards surrounded us, each one a reminder that we were not alone. We could not but be aware that neighbours, friends and family were sharing in our shock and our worry and were concerned, not only for Charlie, but for all of us. It was humbling and uplifting at the same time. You don't often get to appreciate how much most people *care* and we don't usually say a great deal. I made a mental note to try and do better in that department myself.

And another mental note: I remember realising that the images on the cards we received, said more than any words could. Up until then, I'd always wondered whether sending a card to someone in distress was perhaps a bit tacky, and I would agonise over whether to write a proper letter. Now, I could see that in many situations there is absolutely nothing to be said. Words – even the most carefully chosen of words - come out as little more than trite platitudes but pictures speak straight to our emotions. Most of our cards were of the natural world in all its variety, some peaceful, some exuberant, others colourful, others tranquil, and somehow, they were just right. Our lives had suddenly spun out of control but there remained a kind of anchor for us in the amazing beauty and the timeless processes of the earth.

After supper, as the rest of us cleared away, Peter returned every one of the phone calls: from people down the road to relatives in Australia, colleagues in America and friends in France. I don't know how he did it. I was exhausted. I see now he understood more readily than I, that whatever happened, we were going to need support for a long time to come and he took upon himself the thoughtful, practical business of thanking people and keeping them informed. Throughout the evening, passing him mugs of tea, we listened to snatches of conversation and marvelled at the kindness being shown to us. It was late before the last call was completed and Peter was drained as we made our way to bed.

*

One of my favourite Resurrection appearances is the story that begins on the road to Emmaus. It's related by Luke, the writer who continues his gospel into a second volume: *The Acts of the Apostles*. I'm particularly interested in the way he describes how Jesus was first perceived by those who had known him. The narrative begins on Easter Sunday, when early in the morning, the women had discovered the empty tomb. Later that day a disciple called Cleopas set out with another of the brethren to walk to Emmaus, a village about seven miles from Jerusalem. As they walked, they discussed the disastrous events of the past days and the unbelievable tale of the women who claimed to have seen angels. Wrapped in misery, they were joined by a stranger into whose listening ear they poured their troubled disappointment. The stranger did not rush to agree with their gloomy view of things. Instead, he questioned their expectations and their understanding of what had happened. As they walked, the stranger expounded a different view, that the leader, the Messiah they were hoping for, would have offered spiritual, not political, liberation and would have done so not through the exercise of power, but through gentleness and suffering. He reminded them of many teachings from the scriptures that ought to have prepared them for this, and as he spoke, Cleopas and his friend began to see their broken world in a new light. Their hearts were 'on fire' Luke says, as they reached Emmaus and invited the stranger to share a meal with them, and as the stranger broke bread, the realisation dawned on them that their companion was none other than Jesus himself. As soon as they were aware of this, however, the man 'vanished from their sight', leaving them to return, breathless and excited to Jerusalem, to relate what had happened.

I can see that two factors in this story recur regularly in other resurrection appearances. The first is that Jesus was not immediately recognised. Though his followers knew him well, after his death it seemed to take time before they were aware of his presence. And in the same vein, their experience of meeting with him was often fleeting and ended with his disappearance. The disciples were clearly not claiming to have met with a reconstituted, flesh and blood Jesus who lived in the same way as they did. But they claimed, with great certainty, that he continued to exist and had sought them out to reassure and strengthen them.

All this seems both familiar and strange to me. Familiar, in that many people I know to be sane and rational folk, will recount experiences of having been strongly aware of the presence of a loved one who has died. Such experiences are usually powerful and their consequences are enabling, giving the individual much needed courage to carry on through bleak times. But from this common experience we can't conclude that a sensation, however overwhelming, of being *with* someone we know to be dead is anything other than self-delusion or wishful thinking. Yet, unlike other forms of self-delusion, it seems we can't call up this kind of experience through an act of will. (Witness C.S. Lewis who, in *A Grief Observed* laments his inability to feel anything other than fear and desolation at the death of his beloved wife, despite the fact that 'We promised each other we would come back to comfort the other if we could.')

When it happens, it happens in its own time and often in the most unexpected of ways. Like on the road to Emmaus. And what is it? I don't know. But I do suspect this kind of 'presence' is in some way, real.

Am I saying that the Resurrection experiences of Jesus' disciples were essentially no different from those of other bereaved people the world over? I think, yes and no. Yes, because this kind of thing is natural and healing and good and I'm sure Jesus' followers needed and received great sustenance from feelings of renewed closeness to him. No, because although this holds for the early experiences, as time went by, the certainty of being in the company of Jesus of Nazareth gave way to a different kind of experience – that of encountering the Christ of eternity. And now I'm in deep waters!

*

The third day in Intensive Care and we arrived to be told the 'good' news that Charlie was being prepared for another long spell in the operating theatre. My head and my stomach flew into immediate conflict. In my mind I was unequivocally delighted that Charlie's Consultant considered his hold on life to be sufficiently strong to warrant important repair work on both of his arms and detailed investigative surgery to his right leg. But my stomach churned. He was still so vulnerable. His breathing was fragile and would have to be supported throughout. Could they not wait just a little longer? When I tentatively voiced the question, I was gently told that time was of the essence when it came to decision-making about future reconstructive possibilities

– especially concerning his leg. My brain understood but my gut feelings wouldn't be subdued: "Just keep him breathing for God's sake!" I yelled from within: " Never mind his leg!"

But of course, if Charlie was going to pull through – and the signs were good – *he* would mind very much about his leg. He was a young man who loved sport and music and packed his days with activity. If he survived, he would not be content with half measures; he had to be given every opportunity to fight for the best possible level of physical fitness. And the surgeons would never knowingly jeopardise Charlie's survival in their concern for his limbs. All this went over and over through my rational mind. But my stomach kept reminding me that surgery had its own dangers and was never altogether predictable. I simply, selfishly and no matter what, wanted Charlie to live.

They wheeled him away on a trolley and I felt sick. The nurses were brilliant, my family was brilliant and I think I was moderately brave. I resolutely ensured my mind retained the upper hand and I kept myself occupied and talking. Looking back, I can see how protective everyone was of me, and I marvel at their patient goodness. I don't think I was anything like grateful enough at the time.

*

I turn up my coat collar against the wind and hurry down the slope towards the office. My numbed fingers fumble with the swipe card until eventually I hear the locking mechanism click and I push my way through the heavy door and step inside, relieved to be out of the cold. Clutching my overloaded briefcase I stagger up to the first floor and check in with Reception. More doors to be opened with stiff fingers grasping the wretched swipe card, then responding to the warmth beginning to seep into my bones, I greet colleagues with a smile and a reasonably cheerful

"Hello!" I search for a vacant computer to pick up my email. My working day has begun. It won't end until late.

I'm part of the Probation Programmes Team and I have an evening session to run tonight. It's a privilege to work with offenders. I'm not just saying that. As a Probation Officer, of course there are times when I wonder what on earth I'm doing and whether any of it helps. But now and again I know for certain I'm in the right place at the right time for someone. And that's both an awesome responsibility and quite a considerable honour.

Jesus was an offender, when all's said and done. People know this full well from the story of the Passion but they somehow don't think he *counts* as a criminal. After all he wasn't mad or bad or wrong ... was he? But he was considered guilty of blasphemy and sedition; considered so not only by the fickle mob but by the educated elite of Jewish society, entrusted as they were with the day-to-day orderly government of the province.

Jesus was dangerous. And if not he himself, then his followers, with their incomplete understanding and their alarming expectations. And if not his followers, then certainly their impact upon the poor and the downtrodden whose discontent could so easily be stirred up into rebellious frenzy. Neither the Romans nor the Jews could afford that. The Jewish officials who worked with powers grudgingly delegated by their Roman occupiers were constantly alert to the early signs of such disorder and were ready to clamp down hard on any threat.

And really, who could blame them? Only forty or so years later in AD 70 Jerusalem was devastated as a revolt of the Jews was ruthlessly crushed. The Temple was pulled down, many of the Jewish inhabitants of Palestine were dispossessed and large numbers of them scattered. And a second revolt after that sealed the fate of those who'd hung on. It was the Diaspora of a people without a land – unresolved satisfactorily down to our own day. And its roots lie in the tense, edgy society of the time of Jesus. The Jesus who preached challenge and change, no wonder those urbane and clever men charged with keeping the peace were so ready to condemn him. Sedition was a nation-threatening crime and justly or unjustly, Jesus *was* condemned. He wasn't lynched by the mob or secretly assassinated by the authorities; he was brought before the Sanhedrin and the Roman Governor Pilate himself. A threat to his nation, he was considered guilty of a heinous crime. He was beaten, paraded, spat upon and then brutally executed. But according to the judgement of his day, Jesus Christ *was* a criminal.

So I say again, it's really quite a privilege to work with criminals.

*

Returning to Intensive Care after a morning spent fruitlessly wandering around the hospital newsagent's and the medical bookshop, we arrived to see Charlie being wheeled back into his accustomed place. Relief! Both his arms and his right leg were now swathed in smart-looking dressings and seemed more efficiently, more comfortably supported. This small but obvious indication of clinical care and attention to detail was immediately reassuring. For me, this meant that what my mind had already accepted, my stomach could begin to go along with – it could trust these people to use their skills and expertise to do the very best for Charlie.

A bit of a wait whilst the bed was shunted into place and monitors were reconnected and tested. Charlie, still deeply sedated, looked peaceful and tidy – but those smart, careful dressings spoke volumes. They spoke most forcefully of hope but they also spoke of more risk and struggle. For one thing, I could see before I was told, from the way Charlie's mangled right leg was now precisely elevated in its sling, that they had done serious surgical groundwork towards saving it. Great! Of course it was great. But I also knew that now the medical decision to attempt this had been taken, a race against time had already begun. Charlie would have to be strong enough to undergo far longer and more complex surgery than today's – and soon – if possibility were to become reality.

The Consultant took us into a side room and gave us all the time we needed. He'd been operating for hours, must have been dog-tired and I knew he had a wife and young children waiting for him at home. Yet, as we sat and talked, we might have been the only anxious, questioning relatives on the whole of his case-load. He told us, frankly and firmly that Charlie wasn't 'out of the woods' yet. (Oh, those woods! Since the start, every positive piece of news had necessarily been qualified with the phrase 'not out of the woods'.) Even though this was sobering, it was massively important for us to know, for more than anything right now, we needed the truth.

Charlie, he said, had come through surgery well. His injured arms and shoulders were basically functional and though his chest cavity was a mess with all the damage from multiple rib fractures, his lungs seemed to be improving. If he could hold his own now, a step at a time, then plans could be put in place for the future. The first step, he explained, was that Charlie should spend increasing amounts of time off the ventilator. Once he could breathe reliably for himself, they would look to the business of rescuing as much as possible, of his right leg. Below the knee, he told us, the blood supply was precarious and if that wasn't rectified fairly soon, too much tissue would be lost and recon-struction wouldn't be viable. 'Gangrene', I re-worded the problem to myself, 'necrotic tissue', dead, rotting flesh. I almost wished for the clean certainty of amputation. Reading my thoughts, the Consultant gently reminded me that Charlie was a young man with everything to live for. Peter squeezed my hand and not for the first time, his air of quiet confidence re-kindled my own wavering courage.

A step at a time the Consultant had said, but I was unprepared for the rapidity of pace. Back at Charlie's bedside it was clear they were allowing him to re-surface to a higher level of consciousness than before. Every now and then he would groggily open his eyes - beautiful, warm brown eyes - and then close them again. Then he began to focus.

He moved his head on the pillow to survey the group surrounding him: his nurse, me, Peter, Sarah and Tim, and we smiled and said "Hi!" This accomplished on several occasions, the nurse withdrew and, returning with warm water, cotton-wool and a hand-towel, said:

"Charlie, I'm going to wash your face and make you comfortable, OK?"

Charlie directed his gaze at the nurse: "Mmm," he said.

So his face was gently washed and his hair carefully brushed and little by little he grew more aware of what was going on. I joined in and he seemed to enjoy the attention. Working on the opposite side of the bed from the nurse, I laughed as I found a shard of Perspex in his hair from the aircraft, whereupon she discovered another piece in his ear. Then she handed me some cotton buds and asked if I'd like to swab the inside of his mouth and his dry lips. I'd seen this done many times before but not with Charlie being conscious of it, so I was as confident but as gentle as I could be, and somewhat pleased with my performance I enquired:. "How does that feel, Charlie? Good?"

To my astonishment, with a slight shake of his head he forcefully replied: "Naah!"

Shocked, I looked across at the nurse. She was beaming from ear to ear. So was Peter. Sarah and Tim were laughing at my discomfort. Then I grinned too. Charlie was coming back in the fighting form he was going to need. And, oh my, was he going to need it...

* * *

JOY

It seems to me that real, intense joy is not an emotion we experience all that often in our lives. Happiness, eagerness and enthusiasm, well-being, contentment and pleasure, all these are familiar feelings but joy is special. For joy is bound up with its opposites; with sorrow, with longing, with confusion. It feels as though darkness has given way to a flood of light. Optimism, direction and purpose are back on the agenda. Life is for living again! It is not an emotion that lasts but experiencing profound joy can transform the way we look at life for ever afterwards. Not always a comfortable transformation, though, it has to be said.

There's a memorial to the Great War in north London, Finchley, I think, called 'Esprit de Joie'. It's one of the few designed by a woman, and to my mind it encapsulates the explosion of public relief and thankfulness at the longed-for armistice in November 1918. It's not at all martial, not sombre or even, in terms of public art, dignified. It's a sculpture of a young woman, a slender, stylised nude, standing on tiptoes with her outstretched arms flung heavenwards and her head thrown back. Its immediacy and energy is intensely moving. This is what joy *feels* like.

*

The metaphors we use to describe joy don't seem to have changed much over the millennia. We talk about being 'blown away' or 'burning with excitement'. Wind and fire; it brings to mind the Pentecost story, near the start of Luke's second volume: the *Acts of the Apostles*, and here is where I'm going to begin my attempts at *Lectio* properly.

I shan't be able to ponder every single passage in *Acts*, after all, I've only got six weeks, but Pentecost is huge; I have to start here, even though it feels like jumping in at the deep end. Daunting, because though it's certainly a story about joy, I'm sure I'm not the only modern western Christian to feel a trifle squeamish when I read it. For my left brain, schooled in elements of psychology, it smacks too much of hysteria. Perhaps it's the way it's told.

According to Luke, (*Acts 2*) the disciples of Jesus, who'd begun quietly re-grouping back in a house in Jerusalem, were together one morning when suddenly they felt a tremendous force come upon them, overwhelming them, both singly and as a group. There was no hesitation in identifying this joyful and trans-forming experience as a receiving of the power of the Holy Spirit and though this could only be described in metaphor, Luke speaks of it as like 'tongues of fire' resting upon each person, while there was a rushing sound, like a great wind, 'and they were all filled with the Holy Spirit.' Blown away, I guess.

The narration continues dramatically, for straight away an immense, unstoppable surge of confidence crystallised the disciples' thoughts and focused their energies. The effect was as rapid as it was total. Suddenly, the followers of Jesus were back! No more hiding in upper rooms. Immediately, into the crowded Jerusalem streets during the Festival of Weeks, the followers of the executed Jesus burst forth like champagne from a bottle. The analogy is apposite, too, because many in the crowd were afraid they were drunk. They were noisy and excited, all talking at once and their energy was clearly compelling, if disturbing. Were they intoxicated, mad, dangerous?

I think if I'd been there in the streets as an onlooker, I would have definitely assumed all three of the above, and would doubtless have given the disciples a very wide berth indeed. But is it useful, projecting my present self into another time, a different culture and a brilliant but slightly alien way of telling a tale? Goodness, this is my first reading from *Acts* and already I have qualms ...

Firstly, there's this whole thing about a power, beyond

everyday experience, suddenly breaking through into people's lives. It smacks of magic and fairy-tale, it makes me uneasy, and yet ... I have no difficulty accepting that there are times and places where the veil between the everyday and the transcendent can be very thin. Haven't I already recounted how on entering Intensive Care that first, fateful day, I felt a life force, clearly and strongly emanating from Charlie? And my initial apprehension of it was as a force outside myself. It didn't go away, and by the next day I could feel the life force within myself and in everyone I met. It was elemental. Not comforting in an ordinary sense but reassuring in terms of making me feel less small and alone, more a part of something huge, and beyond my understanding. The ability to sense what I perceived as a force, gradually faded as Charlie came back to us and I became involved again in the practicalities of life. Although ... and I hesitate, because I don't want to sound weird ... it's never quite left me. So actually, who am I to doubt the power Luke describes as the Holy Spirit?

Then of course, in my contemporary, individualistic way of seeing things, I worry about the phenomenon of group experience. I'm OK with the idea of people with similar concerns reacting similarly to an unexpected event. I'm OK with the notion of their talking about it, so that very soon they all begin to feel the same way. But a simultaneous group experience? It's not something I recognise ... or do I? Come to think of it, doesn't 'simultaneous experience' exactly describe the power and the magic of live theatre? A singer stands alone, a small figure on a large stage, having sung her heart out to a lover who, it now appears, has betrayed her. She is desolate, and we, the audience, are drawn into her sorrow. All of us, simultaneously. And she holds the moment – long enough to convey its poignancy to the whole audience, but not so long that it becomes sentimental. You can hear a pin drop. And because performer and audience for that moment have become one, the experience is rich, multi-layered, and we are moved.

Yes, I'm describing a contrived phenomenon but it wouldn't be possible to contrive these powerful, theatrical moments were the actuality of group experience not natural to us as humans. And in our western-world way of living as individuals in little boxes marked 'Me' and 'Mine', aren't we the poorer for the pathetic weakness of our group identities?

All right, then, the first part of the Pentecost story is maybe not as strange to me as I think. The private, behind-closed-doors experience of encountering the power of the Holy Spirit, I can get my head around after all. But the next bit still bothers me, the group behaviour bit. Groups in the grip of an emotional 'high' speak danger to me. However joyfully they may begin, there lurks in my mind the possibility of intolerance, anger and violence.

I'm a Probation Officer. I run workshop-type sessions for people convicted of violent offences, and I know only too well that if I strike a disturbing chord with them too forcefully, the whole group will immediately react with defensive, angry resistance.

Amidst the drama and confusion Luke tells how a man stepped forward, silenced the crowd and spoke. It was Peter. The Peter we're all familiar with from the gospels. Peter the bold, impulsive fisherman from Galilee, Peter who denied Jesus thrice and fled to save his skin. But here we have a portrait of a new Peter, Peter the emerging leader. In addressing the crowd, he clearly turned in a strong, level-headed and well-judged perfor-mance. For the throng was calmed and became attentive. Some stayed.

Acts doesn't relate how many of those first curious listeners fell quickly away but what Luke makes clear is that from this time onwards, there existed a reliable nucleus of committed people in Jerusalem, looking to the teachings and example of Jesus to help them live their lives differently. For the disciples, it was an extra-ordinary and courageous 'return to business'.

It strikes me that when we pray in church in a desultory sort of way for the Holy Spirit to transform us, we'd be appalled if anything serious actually happened. And as for something remotely on this scale ... Heaven forbid!

*

Day 4 and with a mixture of excitement and apprehension we drove the short distance to the hospital. Yesterday we'd been able to speak to Charlie. Today, did we dare hope that he might be able to speak to us? We thought of ways to jog his memory and increase his awareness. I put on extra amounts of the perfume I sometimes use, in the hope it would immediately suggest 'Mum' to him, while Sarah and Tim took in some favourite songs to play to him.

He was still groggily surfacing from his drugged night's sleep when we arrived, but as his brother and sister settled in by his bedside, he was clearly listening to their chatter. Peter and I took ourselves off for a coffee and when we returned, Charlie's music was playing. There was less equipment around his bed, he was breathing well for himself and – yes, he was talking. Not much, but "Yes" and "No" in response to questions. Every so often he would drift off into a kind of slumber ... and then the music would bring him back. I remember a ridiculous song that changed key upwards at the end of every verse until it became un-singable, co-written and performed by Charlie himself with a student friend, and how profoundly the magic of laughter lifted everyone's spirits.

Later that morning, as Charlie was washed and then examined by a veritable procession of doctors, we found ourselves repeatedly consigned to the ITU waiting room. Suddenly we were sharing cups of tea with the bewildered relatives of newer, sicker patients than our son. And nothing could have brought our privileged situation of hope home to us half as forcefully as that.

Back at his bedside, we were told that Charlie was indeed

making good progress and could soon be strong enough to make the next step – out of Intensive Care. A Physiotherapist was going to spend some time with him, working on his breathing, so, until he or she arrived, we could encourage Charlie to talk.

It was an effort for him. An effort to concentrate and an effort to form words, but he tried valiantly for us and slowly a kind of conversation emerged as he became able to initiate simple questions:

"What happened?"

"You were flying, remember?"

"Yes."

"In the Cessna, and it crashed. You're in the John Radcliffe Hospital."

"Yes."

"You're in good hands. You're going to be all right."

Then a little later:

"Do you know where you are, Charlie?"

"Hospital."

"That's right. Absolutely right. Do you know why you're in hospital?"

"Crash. … Take-off … crash."

"Yes, you've got it. You're in good hands, you're going to be OK, understand?"

"Mmm."

These and similar exchanges repeated themselves many times, until he was sure. Then he asked the question we'd been half-expecting, half-dreading. He asked what had happened to his flying instructor. .

"We'll find out for you, Charlie." I stalled, as Charlie's nurse took Peter aside:

"There's no point telling him now. He's still so full of drugs he won't remember."

So for the rest of the day, whenever he asked, we repeated that we'd find out – but it was difficult to lie to him.

*

'Two names were put forward.' (*Acts 1: 21-26*) **One of the first things the members of the embryonic Jesus movement actually did was to set about electing a successor to Judas Iscariot. A bold move, I think; forward-looking pragmatic, confident. An impulse to conserve and consolidate would have been perfectly under-standable but this small, dynamic organisation clearly had big ideas from the moment it reaffirmed its existence. This project begun by Jesus in his lifetime, was nothing if not ongoing, and Matthias the new apostle was testimony to that.**

It's something we so easily forget, well, I do. The story of Christianity can seem to focus so much on the past. Yet, in reality, Christian understanding moves continually onwards, tempered by different cultures, re-evaluated in different ages and powered by the energy of man's constant searching, enquiring quest for the transcendent – for God.

*

The Physiotherapist arrived in the afternoon, by which time Charlie was pretty tired. She demanded his concentration – as they do – and, to the best of his ability, he complied. But we couldn't help but feel sorry for him and to begin with, we heartily wished our Physio would go away. However, once he was fixed up to a breathing monitor, we could all see how shallow Charlie's respiration really was. Improving respiratory efficiency and keeping his lungs clear was obviously a priority. Patiently, she cajoled him into a more rhythmical pattern of breathing and encouraged him to extend both inhalations and exhalations until, in a surprisingly short time, the monitor began confirming better results. She was pleased. She even smiled. Heartened by this small success, she placed her hand on his stomach and instructed him to try and lift it with his breathing. He couldn't seem to do it at all. I suspected he didn't have a clue what she meant, so it wasn't quite fair, she wasn't explaining very well. Motherhood is so odd. Here was Charlie in Intensive Care and I was irked that he wasn't being given a proper opportunity to shine.

"Charlie, breathe from your diaphragm," I interjected firmly, with the air of authority I'd just learnt from the Physio herself.

To my great amazement, he did. Having sung all kinds of music from treble chorister days to student rock, he knew all about diaphragmatic breathing. In fact, he was a bit of a star. The monitor shot up with every breath; the Physio was delighted and I was quietly, proudly smug. Motherhood is so odd.

*

I have an infuriating habit of asking people what their jobs actually entail. In my defence, jobs nowadays seem to have such obscure titles. "Yes, but what do you actually *do* all day?" I ask. "I mean, you arrive at work, get a coffee, pick up your email and ... then what?"

Coffee and emails apart, I have some idea (*Acts 2:42-47*) how the early Christians spent their days. They depended heavily on one another, the way survivors do, and they certainly operated very much as a community: praying together, working together, teaching those who would listen and looking after the needy. And, day in, day out, eating together.

Breaking bread. Supper. That cosiest, most ordinary of household events that has, in the Eucharist, the Mass, become *the* central, sacred observance of the Christian Church. Am I the only one, though, who feels that in the gradual but almost total transfer of this gentle ritual from the domestic setting into a 'holy place', something important has been lost?

Judaism is full of special meals, celebrated at home, in the warmth of the love of family and friends, in sharing with guests, in putting out the best china and lighting the Sabbath candles.

And so many of the Resurrection appearances occurred in just this setting, as the disciples gathered to share a meal, at the Emmaus inn, in the Upper Room, by the shore of Galilee.

There is something basic, powerful and sacred about sharing food and drink. It's not awe-inspiring or breath-taking, but earthy and warm and physical. And here is where the disciples first became aware of the Resurrection presence of Jesus; not in the Temple or the Synagogue, not on a mountain-top or in the desert, but at the heart of their everyday existence, when they paused from their labours and put aside their worries to eat together.

Quite different in atmosphere from the ritual the Eucharist has become in institutionalised Christianity. It is, now, awe-inspiring. It is solemn and reverential, ancient and full of layers of meaning, and who would want to tamper with this beautiful office, re-enacted day by day, week by week, in Christian holy places the world over? Not me.

What I'm saying, though, is that in gaining the spiritual nourishment of the Mass, we've gradually lost a profound religious respect for the food that keeps us alive and for the intimacy of food-sharing relationships that were so significant in the ministry of Jesus himself.

We've lost more, I guess, in the 'fat-cat' societies of what we call 'the developed world'. Our superfluity of food has banished hunger, so that most of us have absolutely no understanding of what it *is*. Astonishing when I recall that as a child, many people in post-war Europe were starving, and in London, where I grew up, the poorest still went hungry very often. We have so quickly and utterly forgotten how precious food is, and how great a gift it is to share. So much has changed, so fast, and the spectre of famine in Europe is not something any of us would wish to see again. But our casual snacking, our mass-produced, processed pre-cooked tray-suppers, our greedy, inattentive refuelling in front of the television, our solitary eating under one roof, and the truly horrifying waste of food; this is the closest thing to blasphemy that I know.

Trouble is, I can grumble with the best of them but I know I'm no holier than thou. I was talking with my son Tim the other day about the business of saying grace at meals. Neither of us does it, yet we both feel that just tucking into a plateful of food without even pausing to consider where it came from, who produced it and how lucky we are to be sharing it is – well, it's bad manners to start with, thoughtlessness, but it also impoverishes us, so that eating becomes just another way of exercising consumer choice. Am I a goat cheese salad and cappuccino sort of person or am I burger and chips?

Tim recalled how every meal he ate at school was preceded by a short grace and how a sort of perfunctory gratitude for one's dinner – for boys are perpetually hungry – seemed *right*. For my part, I remembered how my grandmother would make us say a grace before leaving her table. But that was years ago. Nowadays, if I'm invited to eat in a household where grace is still said as a matter of course, I do appreciate it, but I can't help being aware of others around the table who are self-conscious and embarrassed at the whole thing. They lower their eyes and fidget and shuffle their feet – and that's not what I'd want either. I really don't wish my humanist family and friends, whom I delight to feed, to feel uncomfortable or in any way *excluded*. So I don't think I'd want to re-introduce a formal grace to my own table. What, then?

I taught a student once, who, before eating, would simply fold his hands in his lap and pause for a moment. It took a while before I noticed this, and when I remarked upon it he admitted rather shyly that it was just an unobtrusive but effective way of being *attentive*. I liked that and tried to do it myself, but very soon I forgot at the start of the meal and would have to pause half way through, and after that, I started to forget altogether.

Now I serve a meal at table, or receive it in a restaurant, and, before we eat, I wish everyone 'bon appetit'. It always provokes a 'bon appetit' in return and there are usually appreciative remarks about the food. Better than nothing. Better than bunging the food down and everyone just troughing ... but not quite good enough.

*

Charlie slept when the Physio left and we returned home for a while. It was hard to pick up the chores of everyday life but we had to do our best. To be honest, I was hopeless. Cooking and making pots of tea was about my limit while the others bore the brunt of keeping the show on the road. Sarah had to pack to go back to London that evening and would soon have to resume work in Edinburgh. I hugged her so tightly it took her breath away. Tim, working in London, had a bit more flexibility. He volunteered to give her a lift and as the light began to fade at around half past four, they drove off. Peter made a few work-related phone calls. Although I'm a qualified Probation Officer and Social Worker, I was actually occupied at the time in teaching English to foreign students: business and academic. I was in a self-employed phase of life and had just finished a run of work. Under normal circumstances I'd have returned from my break in Paris to get my schedule for the spring sorted out. As it was, however, I firmly blanked out my diary 'until further notice'. My mind was in one place and that was the hospital. Peter and I returned there in the early evening to find Charlie being disconnected from his various machines in readiness for a move.

Oh my Lord! He was being transferred from Intensive Care to the Trauma Ward *that night!* I knew they were planning to move him as soon as he was up to it, but I never envisaged this happening *at night*. Of course, if I'd thought about it, it shouldn't have surprised me that, driven not by the clock, but by a proper medical need, Intensive Care was making room for another patient, more seriously ill than Charlie. They were at pains to explain that they would still be involved with his care during the transfer period and could easily have him back. They told us we weren't to worry if it turned out he couldn't yet manage completely without the ventilator. Many patients, they said, had to return from the Trauma Ward to ITU for a spell before they could finally breathe on their own. But right now, they were optimistic. So we accompanied our son on his journey to the new ward, watching like hawks his every unaided breath.

The Trauma Ward was utterly terrifying. It seemed huge; full of active, importunate patients who would ring their bells and wave their arms to summon the busy nurses who were hurrying this way and that. While Charlie lay still; dependent. He was placed in the observation area, right opposite the nurses' station ... but all the nurses were elsewhere. And although there was an oxygen mask covering his nose and mouth, two drip stands, a catheter bag, and hoists for his right leg and left arm, this was far less equipment than in ITU. Nothing bleeped or gave readings. Charlie seemed naked and vulnerable. Without a breathing monitor, how would the nurses know his respiration was safe? Questions tumbled urgently into my mind but there were no nurses to ask. Where were they?

For the first time, I felt a rising tide of panic. Charlie shouldn't be here, in this noisy, bustling place. He could be overlooked so easily. I was on the verge of angry, frightened tears when suddenly, like magic, a nurse materialised at the bedside. She was short and plump and looked absurdly young, but her eyes were kind and she checked all Charlie's equipment with unhurried efficiency. Even so, it was getting late now and I felt I had only a short time to forge some kind of a bond with her, a bond that would allow me to leave my son in her care overnight. In reality I had no choice, but she was great anyway. She answered all our nervous questions and asked some of her own.

We told her Charlie had been talking a little in ITU, and though his brain was still clearly enmeshed in a morphine-induced muddle, he was making some sense. We then talked for a bit about what she should say if Charlie continued to ask about his flying instructor. Peter and I suspected that somewhere in the back of his mind Charlie already understood his instructor had been killed – after all, he'd slipped in and out of consciousness throughout the rescue.

"Tell him the truth," we decided. And that night, after we left, exhausted but reasonably reassured, he awoke, and asked ... and she told him. He already knew.

*

A crippled man had been healed. Charlie was crippled; that's what initially made me stop at this bit of *Acts (3:1-10, 4:1-22)*. I couldn't help but wonder how the man, already in his forties, used the years that were left to him, but as I could never know that, I read on and was re-immersed in the tense and troubled city of Jerusalem. As the man walked, an excited crowd gathered, whereupon Peter and John, were picked up, brought before the Sanhedrin and called to give an account of themselves.

Luke relates with a certain wry amusement, the surprise of Jewish elders at the poise and confidence of these two 'untrained laymen' from Galilee. Jesus, after all, had been a holy man, versed in the scriptures, but these followers of his were just provincial fishermen. And yet they were informed and articulate as they argued before the Sanhedrin that Jesus of Nazareth was *'the stone rejected by the builders which has become the keystone – and you are the builders'*. And they boldly reminded their listeners of how they had connived and colluded as this extraordinary man Jesus, in whose name the lame could walk, was put to death on a Roman cross.

They weren't shouted down or thrown out. Their audience was attentive and respectful – if unconvinced – and the two disciples were released with a warning to cool it. The idea that the elders of the Jews were baying for Christian blood right from the start is just plain nonsense, and few thinking Christians nowadays will buy that one.

The context into which early Christianity fits – or the thesis that convinces me – is the one that maintains the synoptic gospels (*Mark, Matthew* and *Luke*) and *Acts* were written close to the time, or shortly after the fall of Jerusalem in 70AD. This was a period when relations between the small, progressive Jesus sect and the retrenching mainstream of Judaism were deteriorating fast, but before the followers of Jesus were actually expelled from the synagogues.

So the first narratives we have about the ministries of Jesus and his companions were compiled from the perspective of a radical movement *within* Judaism. And it would seem to have been a movement that in the beginning attracted quite a respectful hearing from the Pharisaic wing of the faith. The next time there were arrests we hear of Rabbi Gameliel's advice to leave the sect alone: '*For if this idea of theirs is of human origin, it will collapse; but if it is from God, you will never be able to put them down.*'

There seem to have been a certain number who were prepared to consider the possibility that Jesus of Nazareth was a prophet as great as Moses or Elijah and that his special mission was not to be a political or military leader, but to be the suffering servant of Israel.

But, arguably, the catastrophic fall of Jerusalem changed everything. The scattered Jews of the Diaspora clung to their religion – it being fundamental to their identity – and as in any siege-type situation, there was less and less room for debaters or fringe groups.

As I understand it, the power of the Temple-based Sadducees was broken as the Temple itself with its (already outdated) sacrificial practices was razed to the ground. Into the vacuum stepped the Pharisees, with their educated Rabbis and their communities around the synagogues. But once in control of Judaism, it seems the Rabbinical schools became more conservative and dictatorial… after all, this was a people determined to survive.

And at this point, the Jesus movement was caught between an increasingly hostile Jewish mainstream and a growing following from among interested Gentiles.

So when Mark, Matthew and Luke wrote, they wrote, I'm sure, as religious Jews, continuing to proclaim the huge importance of Jesus of Nazareth. They made no claims (as were later made) about Jesus that would have been impossible for progressive Jewish thinkers to embrace, and they kept their links with the synagogues wherever they could. Of course, they argued – did they ever! – with a ferocity typical of all representatives of closely competing ideologies, but they remained Jews until the mainstream found them too divisive for the maintenance of cohesion, and threw them out. So the notion that the Sanhedrin at the time of the first Christians was awash with plans to quell the Jesus movement is, I think, ridiculous, a spin administered much later in the Christian day, when it benefited Christians little to be perceived as associated with their Judaic roots.

The Sanhedrin at this point did not feel seriously threatened and some of its members were even rather interested in what the likes of Peter and John had to say. Acrimony certainly did build but who is to say whether there would have been such a decisive split had Jerusalem *not* fallen and the Jews *not* been threatened (again) with national extinction.

Now there's a thought … though it has meandered a long way from the crippled man who made me stop in the first place. I should probably be more disciplined if I aspire to practise *Lectio*. I've always been inclined to push at boundaries – often ruefully to discover they're actually rather helpful.

*

Quite suddenly this morning, the south-westerly wind has returned. I open a small window, breathe, and the air is warm. I go out to collect the milk from the doorstep and I don't shiver.

Wonderful! Even so, the sky remains overcast and the bare branches of the trees are a stark reminder that spring has some catching up to do. It'll still be a while before there's blossom along the Woodstock Road.

I pick up the scruffy diary of Charlie's miracle.

*

Next day on the Trauma Ward, the medical staff seemed very pleased with their new patient. I could see why. Apart from being a genuinely nice fellow, Charlie was sufficiently ill to be challenging and interesting but not yet well enough to have become bad-tempered or demanding. And he was making progress. Though he still spent quite a lot of time in a hazy condition somewhere between sleeping and waking there were increasingly substantial periods when he was awake – and thank God – alert and communicative. His brain had taken one hell of a bashing, but to our huge relief, it was working despite everything.

It was during one of these communicative interludes that I was ejected from Charlie's bedside to make way for a youngish, short, bouncy surgeon called Martin McNally. I was surprised to be asked to give up my chair; then delighted. For, until then, medical decisions had been discussed with Peter and me, but now Charlie was in the driving seat, and quite right too. I couldn't help watching and listening though, and from a polite distance, I got the gist of things.

It was obvious McNally was keen to have a go at rebuilding Charlie's mangled right leg. He produced X-rays and spoke about something I now know is called an Ilizeroff frame. Charlie, propped up on pillows and encumbered by an oxygen mask, nevertheless concentrated intently and began to ask questions. He soon caught the surgeon's enthusiasm for the project and, heads close together, the explanations continued. Then more questions from Charlie, who gesticulated energetically before remembering the backs of his hands were uncomfortably connected to antibiotic and morphine drips. He yelped and let out a rather short word, and they both laughed.

McNally seemed to be saying it was possible to control regenerating bone growth so that slowly, over many months, a shattered bone could be re-grown.

I suppose I should have reacted with: "Amazing!" and "Yes, please!" as Charlie was doing, but all I could focus on was his heavily bandaged right leg. It was so very obviously short – in fact, between the knee and the ankle there just *wasn't* a lot of leg – and all I could think was: "What are the statistics? What are the risks? Will it work? … And if it works, how long will it take? How painful will it be for my son?"

But then I watched as the two of them shook hands, Charlie beaming under his face mask. And *then* I thought: "Yes, amazing! There isn't actually another option. Go for it!"

And so began the daunting work of surgery, of getting-over-surgery, of hitches and getting-around-hitches, of unrealistic hopes and equally irrational fears. It would be a very long time before anything resembling calm was on the menu.

So it's probably just as well that as I watched Charlie shake McNally's hand, clairvoyance was not my strong suit.

* * *

WORK

We cannot remain in a state of joy indefinitely. Hopefully, having known it, we'll never forget how amazing it feels, but life with all its petty problems has to be lived. We must work. Make up for lost time. Repair what is broken. Try and look towards the future.

After a miracle, work seems comforting. It is concrete, it is satisfying; it occupies and tires but at the same time it is, in emotional terms, relatively undemanding. It just needs to be got on with. But it's so easy to kid yourself you're bravely 'back at the helm' when the truth is, you're still high on natural 'speed', swinging wildly between bold creativity and fearful caution. That was certainly me. Work was something I tackled uncertainly, unevenly and with hugely varying results.

And that's what's extraordinary for me about *Acts*. It's all there. In tracing the story of the earliest Christians and what they did with their lives after the shattering events of Easter, I feel a real closeness to them. I readily enter into their excitement and their determination, their supportive friendships and the damaging divisions I know are in the offing. For though joy inspires and energises, it doesn't direct. Picking up the reins of daily life again, we have to solve our own problems. No Holy Spirit is going to do it for us, nor prevent us from making mistakes. Navigating my way through the *Acts of the Apostles* in tandem with my scruffy diary, I have an immediate sense of understanding, and oddly, a sense that across time, I too, am *understood*.

*

Spring is back on track! The blossom is coming out at last, and soon the Woodstock Road will be transformed into a pink and white processional route for commuters into the city. The banks on the Marston Ferry Road are heavy with daffodils in bud, and primroses and crocuses are beginning to bloom alongside the snowdrops. It's a relief.

I suspect there exists a primitive fear that one winter the sun might depart for ever. Obviously, I don't recognise this as a thought in my conscious mind, but the fact I do feel relief that spring is arriving, suggests I may well have feared it wouldn't, somewhere deep in my *un*conscious. A land gripped in perpetual winter with no warmth, no new life, no new growth, no renewed hope: that's the stuff of primitive religion.

The concept of propitiating the gods to ensure the smooth arrival and departure of the seasons is familiar enough, and it's not hard to see why. The need to end the parched, burning ascendancy of summer as the harvest is brought in, is as pressing as its counterpart, when the barren period of winter needs to give way to spring. This, to facilitate the cycle of planting, growth, harvest and fallow – the cycle that allows man to eat and survive and reproduce. The cycle of life itself.

We don't attempt to propitiate the gods any longer, though I think my Book of Common Prayer still contains intercessions for the relief of drought, dearth, plague and so forth. Nowadays, we no longer hold a divine being accountable for 'acts of God' and accept that it's really down to us to seek and implement remedies for natural disasters.

But we remain creatures moulded, conditioned and supported by the cycles of our everyday experience. The cycle of the day: sunrise, going to work, returning home, sunset, rest and then another day. The cycle of the year with its feasts and seasons: Christmas, New Year, Lent, Easter, summer holidays, Halloween/ Bonfire Night and then Christmas again. The cycle of an individual life: birth, youth, maturity; play, study, work and family; age, dependency, death and then, perhaps another start of some sort.

Spiritually, I tend to think that whatever it is we essentially are, it is not extinguished at our death, though in what manner or to what degree we may continue to exist thereafter, I cannot imagine. It will surely be as memories and in genes and, physically, as some very basic components of the universal soup, but I rather hope for something else as well. What else? I don't know, but I'm speculating it has something to do with our deeper levels of consciousness. For example, I'm aware that when I'm communicating really effectively with another person, or sometimes when I'm teaching a group of people, I'm actually not interacting at the 'me' level of my being but at the 'us' level ... the 'us' level of our being. My experience is not unique to me. Others understand it, others can participate in it: there is something of me in you and of you in me. I don't think that's weird, I think that's how nature is. And if existence beyond individual physical death should occur at a universal level, I should be well pleased.

*

Day 2 on the Trauma Ward and Charlie was deemed fit enough to be visited by the Air Accident Investigation Board. It was important that they talked to him as soon as possible for, as they explained, our minds hate gaps in narratives and without our willing it, make up the bits we can't remember, so strongly do we require a coherent whole on which to reflect.

The bedside interview was led by an experienced female pilot. Charlie said afterwards she was brilliant: unhurried and sensitive, not pushing him, not commenting on his answers, but gently encouraging and repeatedly thanking him. It was a heavy, serious business.

Charlie found he could remember the lead-up to the accident in great detail, right up to the moment when the Cessna's nose abruptly went down ... and then no more. Not the headlong plummeting to the ground, not the impact, and none of the moments of consciousness during his rescue. He remembered nothing more, in fact, until the disconnected thoughts and bizarre dreams of his time in Intensive Care. But going through the events of his flying lesson in minute detail – several times – was actually good for Charlie. It allowed him not only to order his thoughts and be sure what was real at an early stage in his recovery, it also enabled him to feel more confidently in control of his thoughts and emotions. In a situation where he remained physically helpless, this experience of being listened to, of performing a socially important task that only *he* could perform, and of confronting the disaster in a calm and methodical fashion ... was a huge step back towards selfhood.

*

Work, tasks, leadership. I've got to the appointment of deacons *(Acts 6:1-7)* and the whole thorny issue of effective leadership, if a job is to be done. How would the immediate followers of Jesus have seen their job? I guess in broad terms they'd have defined it as being to spread the teachings of Jesus of Nazareth, teachings by word, deed and lived example, to those of Jewish faith and also to 'God-fearing' Gentiles.

I ask myself: "Did Jesus intend to form a religious movement?" Some people deny it, but it seems to me he did. I think it likely that from a historical perspective, Jesus the teacher, aimed to initiate a movement to revitalise Judaism from within and possibly to take its essential precepts beyond the boundaries of the Jewish community. For me, the fact that he called and carefully mentored disciples demonstrates he was serious about challenging certain aspects of mainstream Judaism. Even though he was clearly a charismatic personality, he was not content to be a 'one man band'. He was organised and focused and determined to get his message across to all who would listen – and that did entail forming a movement, however small.

It seems the disciples, too, believed there was a job to be done. Jesus was not just a holy man who had tragically died, but a man of his time, with a message of the utmost importance. Very soon after Easter they demonstrated their commitment to the ongoing mission of Jesus by bringing another apostle into their inner circle to fill the gap left by Judas Iscariot. They clearly felt compelled to take the spiritual teaching they had received to others who wanted to partake of it. However, expansion, even of modest proportions, was never going to be trouble-free.

Leadership obviously lay with a small group of rural Galilean Jews, culturally somewhat different from the Judeans who populated Jerusalem and significantly different from the Hellenised (Greek speaking) Jews who came and went from the city from all over the Mediterranean basin. And while *Acts* takes up the Christian story *after* the disciples had chosen not to return to Galilee but to remain in Jerusalem to further their mission, it also records how, right from the start there were tensions between the different elements that made up the embryonic church. No surprises there then, I'd say – but I live in a world riven by hugely dangerous cultural misunderstandings, so I tend to regard them as inevitable.

Back to the early church. It seems the Greek speaking newcomers to the Jesus movement fairly soon began to grumble that they were receiving less favourable treatment than their Aramaic speaking, Palestinian brethren. They had much to contribute but they were excluded from the councils of leadership and the widows and orphans amongst them were being neglected. All credit to the twelve apostles, who grasped the nettle as best they could. They acknowledged that there'd been organisational failures and invited the Greek-speakers to choose seven of their number to act in an important new capacity, as deacons. Deacons would oversee the general welfare of the community and in so doing, would free the apostles to concentrate on teaching and spiritual leadership. Shared responsibility; in theory.

In practice, it reads to me that, in solving the problem, the first step in an official hierarchy was rather hastily created. For although the deacons embraced their remit with an enthusiasm and commitment that went well beyond what was asked of them, their successors came to bear the status of 'second tier' officers: ordained, but not to the priesthood. The first seven deacons shouldered a heavy responsibility as representatives of their group and must have keenly felt the need to prove themselves worthy. It couldn't have been easy, being new kids on the block.

And from the disciples' point of view, welcoming in the newcomers must have taken courage. They did so because the mission took precedence, and division of labour with selection by aptitude was required if the job was to be done.

And yet, and yet ... The words of Jesus ring out, blessing the outcasts, the poor and the meek: 'The last shall be first'. Would he have wanted to found a movement with a complicated hierarchy and exclusions against certain types of people holding office?

On the other hand it's a fact that as social animals we look for leaders and we scramble and scrap for status, and if the Jesus movement was to expand, it was going to have to live in the real world. It would need to choose leaders who could command the respect necessary to take the mission forward – and they wouldn't be beggars or prostitutes or tax collectors and they certainly wouldn't be meek.

*

In the real world, momentum matters. If a problem has to be solved you can't stand around for ever, debating the details.

I'm astonished, because I look at the scruffy diary of the accident and I see that Charlie was moved from the Trauma Ward later that

same day: *Morning. Air Accident Investigation ...* Then, further
down the page: *Afternoon. To Radcliffe Infirmary.*

At this distance in time, I would have sworn he spent a good
four or five days on the Trauma Ward, perhaps because the short
period there was packed with noise and colour and incident.
Maybe it registered so strongly because it was such an abrupt and
frightening contrast to Intensive Care. On reflection, he *couldn't*
have been there long, since Mr McNally's bid to reconstruct his
leg depended entirely on his having a potentially healthy limb to
work with, and, lacking a useful blood supply, the tissue in
Charlie's right leg was dying by the day.

The Radcliffe Infirmary, at the city end of the Woodstock
Road, was actually closer to where we lived than the John
Radcliffe, but the parking was dire. Visiting entailed the ghoulish
strategy of spotting departing patients in their wheelchairs, or
elderly, slow-moving visitors, and shadowing them to their cars,
with engine running and foot hovering over the accelerator in
order to beat any competition into the forthcoming parking place.

It's gone now, the Radcliffe Infirmary; relocated to the John
Radcliffe site. Better buildings, heaps better parking, but I still
turn and peer in through the gateway at the elegant 18th century
entrance to the Infirmary, every time I pass it, and my heart skips
a beat as the shades of a hundred different emotions still make
their presence felt.

Once there, on the ward named after the plastic surgeon,
Professor Kilner, Charlie immediately faced an exhausting round
of examinations, investigations, explanations, scans and X-rays.
But he coped. He was being pumped full of an alarming number
of drugs to control infection, pain and inflammation, but he was
rapidly getting stronger. Most importantly, he was beginning to
breathe for longer and longer periods without the oxygen mask,
so that the risk he would need emergency intervention with his
breathing during surgery was receding. A short investigative
operation was planned for the next day with a much longer one

in prospect if things looked good.

*

Melissa, as I said before, had found out about Charlie's accident when she phoned cheerfully from her job in Italy to wish him a Happy Birthday.

Charlie and Melissa, Melissa and Charlie; they'd had a volatile yet inseparable relationship right through their school sixth-form. After that, they'd kept in touch, despite going to different universities and dating numerous other girlfriends and boyfriends. When they did meet up they laughed a lot … the chemistry undoubtedly remained.

She'd been horrified by the news and was determined to get back at the earliest opportunity to see for herself that her old flame was alive and kicking – even if he was far from being in one piece. She arranged cover and travel, a flying visit, arriving at the hospital on the day Charlie was due to have the final exploratory operation that would give or withhold the go-ahead for limb reconstruction.

We walked together into Charlie's side-room off Kilner Ward, Melissa tense but resolved – she hated hospitals. There he was, propped up in bed, under a 'Nil by Mouth' sign, awaiting the call for theatre – not the happiest of prospects – but his face lit up like the Blackpool illuminations when he saw her. I left them as they wordlessly embraced and went to get a cup of tea.

When I came back into the room she was sitting on the bed, carefully avoiding the drips and tubes, and she and Charlie were laughing together – youthful and optimistic – as though nothing of any great import had happened, or could happen, or was going to happen. They were relaxed and assured in one another's company, needing no time to adjust to absence and making no demands.

We'd been told Charlie would probably be one of the first on the list for theatre that day, so every time any staff came near us, we jumped in anticipation – only to subside as we realised they were about other business. The day wore on. Obviously, the surgeons had rearranged their provisional order, but word came through that Charlie would still be seen and that, beyond tiny sips of water, it was still 'nil by mouth' for him. I came and went, bringing back tea and biscuits for Melissa. Nerves produced gales of laughter at the blackest of humour while Melissa re-ordered the muddle of Charlie's get-well cards, his locker, his washing and shaving kit, his pile of bad-taste T shirts – and the banter between them continued non-stop.

It was 4 o'clock in the afternoon when they finally came for him. Two friendly porters expertly transferred Charlie to a trolley, and, almost before we knew it, he was waving to us, disappearing down the corridor. As their clatter and footfalls echoed and died away, the awfulness of what the surgeons were going to decide could be ignored no longer. Melissa and I exchanged a helpless look and fell sobbing, great, noisy, pent up sobs, into one another's arms.

*

I see I wrote in my diary: *We all feel like peeled prawns.* By that, I meant we'd lost our defences. We had no choice but to live from day to day, tossed from one emotion to the next: from hope to anxiety, to joy, to gratitude, as helpless as children. Our everyday mental filters of reason and common-sense, expectation and habit had been blown apart by events beyond our control, leaving us open as never before.

Sometimes I still feel like that - undefended - but not so often. Sometimes I'm quite staggered by the beauty of sunlight on water, or the drumming of raindrops, or the casual kindness of a stranger. Sometimes a small disappointment or a sharp remark can bring tears to my eyes that are quite unwarranted, but hard to fight back. And I remember those weeks – months actually – when I lived with defences so low that everything got through to me.

Is that what Jesus had in mind when he said: 'Unless you become like children you will never enter the kingdom of Heaven'? I guess for adults, with the burdens of everyday existence pressing on their shoulders it was as hard to be open and childlike then, as it remains now.

*

It's a terrible story, the martyrdom of Stephen. *(Acts 6:8-15, 7:1-60)* Were they asking for trouble or would it have happened anyway? The new, Greek-speaking Christians, rushing to take the message of Jesus into their own synagogues and stirring up heated debate. It was Stephen the Deacon who was arrested.

We know how it went. Hauled before the Sanhedrin, Stephen defended himself with verve and scholarship. There's no mention of a judgement or a sentence and in any case the Sanhedrin had no power to put anyone to death ... but it happened anyway. A stoning: a horrible, bloodthirsty, barbaric lynching. And Stephen in the midst of it all, praying: "Lord, lay not this sin to their charge." Goodness knows how long it lasted, but when it was all over, a few brave friends took it upon themselves to gather up the broken body, and give Stephen a decent burial.

Reading this makes me feel deeply uneasy, for the event as written is a powerful evocation of fear. Fear in the onlookers to the trial who couldn't stomach Stephen's being given a platform for his despicable views. And fear afterwards in the whole Christian community as the reality of Stephen's death sunk in. Fear amongst conservative Jews of this alarming Jesus movement – and within that movement, one senses a certain uneasy fear too.

The story makes no mention at all of the Galilean apostles, it's a 'Greek' narrative. It tells of Stephen, the newcomer: a Greek-speaker taking a lead, taking a risk, taking the consequences. Up till now the Galileans had made all the running, but the 'Way of Christ' was nothing if not dynamic, and change was never going to be comfortable.

*

Or am I being over-dramatic? Perhaps it's because I'm at a place in the scruffy diary where fear was a nagging constant, so I know all too well how difficult is the struggle to keep it in check. For Charlie, amputation at this stage would have been desperately hard, but the medical processes in motion were quite outside our control. What to do?

Keep going, keep hoping, keep working, keep the momentum.

*

In the city centre, the traffic lights outside the Radcliffe Infirmary turned red and a motley crew began a slow crossing of the road. A young man in a wheelchair, another pushing him, a third and fourth wheeling drip-stands and yet more young friends behind and before. Add parents and a couple of grandparents and it was quite a Sunday lunchtime procession, heading for the Royal Oak pub on the further side of the road.

Charlie, white as a sheet but sitting up straight in the chair, clasping his catheter-bag underneath a blanket, was guest of honour. Car drivers, remaining stationary despite the green traffic light, waved and smiled enthusiastically and we returned the gesture. It took ages for us all to get from one side of the highway to the other, while the traffic built and queued embarrassingly. Worth it though.

The doctors at the Infirmary had said that Charlie might as

well try and get out for lunch, The Royal Oak, they told us, was used to their patients. And as the following day was going to see the start of their attempt to save and then rebuild his right leg, there'd be no more outings for many months.

They gave us a side-room and we, a noisy gaggle of Charlie's supporters, settled down with Charlie himself ensconced at the head of the table. In front of him was a hearty platter of something-and-chips and at his elbow was a pint of beer. In truth, he wasn't able to eat or drink very much at all, but that wasn't the point. It was a defiant gesture of intent. Despite the ghastliness of the repeated surgery everyone knew was coming, he was going to stay the course … and his family and friends were going to walk with him, as many steps of the way as were humanly possible.

*

Faith is an odd thing, isn't it? We had faith in the doctors who were going to operate on Charlie – but of course that didn't mean we expected everything to go without a hitch. We knew full well that every stage in the procedures planned for him came with risk and pain attached. So what did our faith consist of, then? I suppose it was about *trust;* trusting the surgeons whose knowledge and skill and experience we understood would be used always and only in Charlie's best interests.

And *trust* is pretty much what I take faith in God to be about. Not, for me, a hope that some 'higher being' is taking care of things. And not, for me, a blind belief in other people's definitions of God (I can't do that either – as a child of my time, my mind cautions me against accepting propositions that require proof 'on trust' from others.)

No, faith for me has to be trust in my own experience. Does that sound arrogant? It isn't meant to be, because my own experience is so very slender and I'm only too aware that my faith is a puny creature beside the confidence of others. But it's all I have to work with, and in a sense, aren't we all agnostics? For when it comes to God, none of us really *knows* what we're talking about. And the older I get, the more comfortable I become with *not* knowing. The bendy sapling willow that is my faith suits me better than a solid old oak.

*

In a seven hour operation, three of Charlie's 'six-pack' stomach muscles were removed and painstakingly transplanted into his right leg, between knee and ankle. The aim was to give him a mass of healthy tissue to provide a proper blood supply to his foot and to create an environment in which the fractured ends of his shin bones might re-grow – if it worked. Oh, and while the surgeons were at it, there was also skin grafting to cover other injuries. And then a nail-biting wait of days: days for Charlie to recover from the ordeal, and days for the transplanted tissue to settle and hopefully to 'take'.

Melissa had to return to Italy – her contract ran until Easter. Charlie missed her but tried to make light of it. After all, they weren't 'an item', just good friends, and he needed support and companionship from everyone who knew him. They all came. Day after day his hospital side-room was filled with raucous laughter as mates from university and school and colleagues from various vacation jobs turned up to keep him company. Heaven knows how the nursing staff put up with it, but it was just what he needed.

*

I was there when they took the bandages off his leg to look at the transplant. As they were unwound, the strips of bandage were increasingly bloodstained and smelly. My heart began to sink as I feared the surgery had been in vain and we would eventually be faced with – well, rotting flesh. The last pieces of gauze were slowly, carefully removed … and I could hardly believe it! There revealed was a very large piece of shining red meat – like rather good steak. Fantastic!

Charlie, it has to be said, was less than thrilled with its butcher's shop appearance but I was ecstatic:

"Look, look! It's healthy!" I cried, much to the amusement of the nurse doing the unwinding, who, though pleased, could see with Charlie that his leg was not a thing of beauty.

*

'The witnesses laid their coats at the feet of a young man named Saul.'
(Acts 7: 58)

This portentous statement introduces into the story of the early church, the towering figure of St Paul. I'm pleased to meet him. Not that he does much towering to begin with. Here, at the stoning of Stephen, Saul is an approving onlooker. I wonder whether he played some part in getting Stephen arrested? I certainly read that, immediately after the appalling lynching, Saul was active in *'harrying the church … seizing men and women and sending them to prison'*. And, of course, the next time I hear of him, he's on his way to Damascus to continue doing just that.

So, was I mistaken in thinking that in the beginning, the Sanhedrin was relatively relaxed about the Jesus movement?

Speaking as someone whose first favourite subject was history, I'm already finding this reading of *Acts* fascinating. For Luke's assertion that the embryonic church suffered *persecution* following Stephen's death begs some questions. There certainly seems to have been trouble for the Jesus movement at this time – but trouble for all of them? There's no mention of Peter or John being picked up (though the authorities clearly knew where to find them) and no suggestion that any of the apostles went into hiding.

Stephen's colleague and fellow deacon, Philip, fled Jerusalem in the aftermath of the tragedy and began a fruitful mission in Samaria. Meanwhile, Saul, from his own account as well as Luke's, took up a hunt for dangerous Jewish deviants with gusto.

This, perhaps, furnishes some clues about the nature and extent of the troubles. For the young Saul, zealous though he undoubtedly was, scarcely represented 'the heavy mob'. Some people think he may have been a very junior member of the Sanhedrin, but even if that were so, he would have had little power and few resources at his disposal. He would have been heartily disliked by those he sought, and those he sought seem to have belonged to the Greek rather than the Aramaic-speaking element of the early church.

From the hearing against Stephen to the Damascus journey, Saul appears to have been involved in a low-level but officially countenanced 'shot across the bows' of the Greek-speaking Christians. Or that's how I understand it. Luke, the 'evangelist to the Gentiles' would indeed have viewed this move against the Diaspora Christians (though at this time they would all have been religious Jews) as the first persecution of the church, led, ironically, by one of its greatest future members.

This version of events, if close to the truth, is interesting, because it suggests that pretty much from Stephen onwards, the Greek-speakers had a distinctive story of their own. And, picking up on the tension I sensed earlier, I wonder if this was already presenting a challenge to the Galilean apostles whose formidable task it was to lead and hold the Jesus movement together?

But back to the scruffy diary ...

*

... And unease is a theme here too. After a week or so of steady progress, they moved Charlie from his side-room into the main ward. From a medical point of view this was clearly 'onwards and upwards' but for him, it was psychologically testing. It was an old-fashioned 'Nightingale' ward: a long narrow room with beds in line all the way down. Charlie was fortunate in being at the far end, next to a window, so he could sit propped up in bed and at least see into the yard beyond. The nurses were as kind and attentive as they could be, but of course he didn't require or receive quite as much attention as before.

His visitors now had to behave with decorum, so as not to interfere with others, and the other patients included a number who were curious and talkative. Charlie, although not averse to conversation, tired easily and we often arrived to find the curtains drawn around his bed. We had lived with optimism and grown accustomed to success, but it was suddenly clear how very ill he still was.

Whether it was his fragility that made me decide not to mention it, I don't remember now, but it was a mistake. It was the day of his flying instructor's funeral – much delayed due to the grim necessity for a post mortem. Peter steeled himself to go; I simply wasn't brave enough. Towards lunchtime, I went in to the hospital and Charlie didn't bring up the subject - though he'd been told about it a day or two before. We chatted inconsequentially and from time to time gazed out of the window in companionable silence. The funeral was due to begin at 1 o'clock and so, when Charlie's lunch arrived, I left him to eat and took myself off to the hospital chapel, there to sit in silence for a while.

I could hardly bear to think. I wondered how the parents were coping, how Peter was coping, how anybody copes, ever, with the death of a child. I felt small and undeserving of our miracle and more sad but more fiercely grateful than words could say.

When I returned to Charlie's bedside, he'd asked for the curtains to be drawn around him. I found him sitting, hunched, staring into the middle distance; his lunch untouched.

We looked at one another and he said: "The funeral, Mum."

"I know," I replied, feeling sick.

How could I have left him? How could I have imagined he'd forget? How could I have let him down on this terrible day? In two strides I was by his side. I took him in my arms and he wept.

*

I've got to that colourful story about the encounter of Philip the Deacon with the Ethiopian eunuch. *(Acts 8:26-40)*

It happened in the middle of nowhere – on the desert road between Jerusalem and Gaza - the high official of the Queen of Ethiopia in his carriage meeting Philip, who was presumably on foot. The great man had been on a pilgrimage to Jerusalem and he was reading aloud from a scroll of Isaiah. Philip, not one to miss an opportunity, approached the carriage and engaged the man in conversation. In no time Philip was sitting beside him, explaining that the suffering servant of Israel of whom he read, had lived and died amongst them and was one Jesus of Nazareth. He talked and listened until the Ethiopian was filled with excitement about this Jesus.

As they came upon some water the Ethiopian asked if there were any reason he couldn't be baptised then and there - and finding none, Philip baptised him.

There's a lot of baptising in *Acts*, which is interesting, because it doesn't seem from the gospels as though Jesus went in for it much. Of course, he underwent the ritual himself at the hands of John the Baptist, and many think that, as a younger man, Jesus may well have been one of his disciples.

John's baptism seems essentially to have signified a cleansing – a washing away of sin in preparation for the beginning of a new era in the relationship between God and man.

At some point after his own baptism, the gospels relate how Jesus left John's circle and set about preaching a message of 'the kingdom of heaven' in his own way.

Apart from a passing reference in *John*, suggesting that Jesus was soon 'winning and baptising' more followers than his erstwhile mentor, the narratives of Jesus' ministry include not a single account of Jesus actually doing so. He isn't likely to have repudiated the practice, it seems he remained deeply respectful of John and all he stood for. Furthermore, in continuing the work of Jesus after his death, the apostles baptised new members of their community, right from the start. They certainly wouldn't have done that if Jesus had deliberately set his face against it. But it seems that the significance of the apostles' baptism had changed its emphasis from that of John. It still symbolised a cleansing of sin, but the new life this entailed from baptism onwards, appears to have been envisaged within a tight community of believers and came to be seen as nothing less than spiritual rebirth.

It's interesting that the rite of baptism still provokes argument and controversy amongst Christians today. Whilst accepting all three elements of this sacrament (cleansing from sin, entering a Christian community, and being 'born again') Christians disagree over the detail. There are many who consider baptism should be reserved for adult converts, even those who were raised in Christian households, for they believe it is vital that each baptised individual should experience a new birth into a new life for themselves.

There are many more, however, who embrace the tradition of infant baptism, which had its origins in the days of persecution. For them, the public declaration that this new child is, by right, a member of the Christian community is paramount.

And the argument continues. My children were baptised and I remember their baptisms with great happiness. But what about the many parents in today's secular society, who want the beauty and solemnity of a church baptism for their child, to welcome him or her into a loving family set in a wider community – but who have not the slightest intention of returning to church afterwards? This scenario's undoubtedly a watering-down of the original purpose of baptism but if, today, one accepts there is a real need that a Christian ritual can legitimately answer, should it be withheld?

Surely baptism never was a 'magic bullet' and there were always people, some, I think, mentioned in *Acts*, for whom it did not make the huge spiritual difference they'd hoped for in their lives.

Anyway nowadays, some parents are given the christening they ask for, others are offered a 'naming ceremony' and still others are refused anything at all unless they demonstrate a minimal commitment to the faith of the church. Me? I'd go with the baptisers. A ritual, after all, is only an outward sign of a deeper conviction, and who are we to judge and exclude?

*

Another week and it was clear the amazing micro-surgery at the Infirmary had 'taken'. Charlie now had a right leg, even though rather a lot of it had formerly been stomach muscle. It was time for him to return to the Trauma ward at the John Radcliffe. We met up with him there in the afternoon, and settling back in, he grinned and told us how his image had just suffered a dent.

It seems the two paramedics who stretchered him out from the Infirmary to the ambulance had heard he'd survived an aircraft crash. They duly bombarded him with questions and Charlie, responding to expectations, replied in the nonchalant manner that he thought a trainee pilot should. As they loaded him into the ambulance, however, he was greeted by the sudden sight of the spring blossom along the Woodstock Road; drifts of pink and white that lined the route they were about to drive. Having been cooped up in hospital with its indoor reality, he gasped audibly at the sight, burbling: "Oh! Wow! It's beautiful!" Not the cool, macho image he'd been cultivating a moment or two before.

*

A short time back at the John Radcliffe and Charlie was once again into major surgery. In another horribly long operation, Martin McNally fitted the promised Ilizeroff frame – and then there were days of recovery.

It had the appearance more of a feat of basic engineering than of a high-tech product of the computer age. The halo frame on Charlie's leg looked crude and heavy and if you stared too long at the wires passing through his flesh, it was, frankly, gruesome. In fact, though, the Ilizeroff frame was titanium-light and its network of wires made precision adjustment possible. And adjustment was what it was all about.

We were told the purpose of the frame was to hold the severed ends of Charlie's shin bones absolutely firmly and very closely together. The bones would then grow, in an attempt to meet and join but the frame would be fractionally adjusted, day by day to keep the bones slightly apart and still growing. By this means it was hoped that enough new bone could be generated to restore his lower leg to its proper length.

In the beginning, while Charlie recovered from the surgery, the minute adjustments to the frame were done for him, but a few days later he was given a spanner, a training session and step by step instructions on the back of an envelope – well, I think it was actually the back of a 'get well' card. From then on, he was responsible for keeping the frame and the 'pin sites' (where the wires exited through his skin) clean, and for making the regular, frequent quarter-turns to the numerous nuts that allowed the Ilizeroff to fractionally extend. It was an amazing piece of kit. Crucially for bone growth in the long term, it was weight-bearing – though Charlie's other injuries left him in no condition to take immediate advantage of this.

For a little while he struggled to get on top of things; two major operations had left him groggy, sore and, despite medication, in significant pain. But he remained determined – for he now possessed real hope that eventually he would stand and walk again on his own two feet.

*

Samaria, the maps in the back of my New English Bible confirm, was the chunk of inland territory between Galilee and Judea. I gather its inhabitants were racially mixed, the region having been conquered and colonised by the Assyrians several centuries before. Hebraic culture survived, however, and the dominant religion of the area was Judaism, but a variant of Judaism considered by the mainstream to be heretical and schismatic. Hence the sharp animosity towards Samaritans evident in the gospel stories.

Anyway, *Acts (8: 4-8, 14-17)* relates how Phillip took flight to Samaria after the stoning of his colleague, Stephen, and – when not approaching stray Ethiopians in the desert - began preaching the message of Jesus there.

It seems to have proved fertile ground. Apparently, the Samaritan concept of the Messiah had tended to be more that of a prophetical teacher than a military leader, and of course, Jesus the man accorded well with this notion. Moreover, bearing in mind the account of his lengthy discussion with the Samaritan woman at the well and the beautiful parable of the Good Samaritan, it's perfectly possible Jesus was already known in Samaria.

So Phillip did well. He was clearly a powerful and persuasive speaker, *Acts* recounts crowds and miracles and great numbers coming forward for baptism. He was doing so well that we're told the apostles in Jerusalem sent Peter and John to join him for a time. And it's good to be reminded of the basic solidarity between the 'new' and the 'old' leaders of the movement, a reassurance that they were all pointing in the same direction. And it was suddenly with the arrival of Peter and John amongst the fledgling

Christians that people began to experience for themselves a profound understanding that what they were committing themselves to, was real. Or as Luke says, they 'received the Holy Spirit'. It wasn't that Phillip was inadequate – far from it - rather that Peter and John were exceptional. For people who may have been converted 'en masse' it seems that it was being with the inspirational apostles Peter and John that really made their baptism into the new beginning it symbolised.

*

We've all met amazing people, now and again. I mean, good people. Warm, loving, caring people; funny, clear, unburdened people; calm, thoughtful, prayerful, happy people. And when our lives touch theirs, we are enriched. We cannot help ourselves wanting whatever that certain something is that they have. Often, it turns out to be a deep spiritual conviction, pursued with quiet discipline. And we're impressed .... but it's too hard for us. We miss out and we know it, but we're too busy already, and it's altogether too much to ask. We want rewards, not toil. We want our faith to be convenient – more than a peripheral interest but less than our whole way of life.

* * *

GRIEF

Then he was ill. Frighteningly so. During the course of a morning Charlie's breathing became uncomfortable – first a little, then more so – until every inhalation caused him pain. The nurses upped his analgesic and told him not to worry, but by lunch time he was no better. In the afternoon Tim sat quietly with him as he battled grimly with the pain of every breath. By now his laboured breathing was beginning to scare us, and at our request, two junior doctors on duty came to look at him.

Tim, joined by a visiting Aunt and I, awaited their verdict. When it came, it was that Charlie was not in any danger and was probably exacerbating his condition by being anxious. Message: we should all chill out.

We were utterly unconvinced. The ultimate helplessness of the sick was brought home to us as we watched the two well-intentioned, white-coated young doctors turn their backs and walk away. Our anxiety was rising, but resolving not to communicate this to Charlie, we temporarily went our separate ways. I took myself off to the cafeteria to think, while our visitor had to go home, promising to come back. Only Tim quietly, solidly remained at Charlie's bedside.

When I returned, Charlie's breathing was clearly worse, and Tim, though still a calm, quiet presence, looked at me meaningfully, as if to say: "Something has to be done." Without more ado, he and I forcefully approached the nursing station and at our insistence, the ward sister came, looked, and acknowledged the deterioration.

Charlie's breathing was now shallow and his face was contorted with pain. A Registrar came immediately, trailing a string of House Officers. His examination was quick but methodical and he talked all the while to his entourage.

Amongst the possible causes of the problem I heard the words 'pulmonary embolism' and my heart skipped a beat. So far, Charlie had escaped on-going heart and lung problems, despite his lack of intact ribs. Though both lungs had been punctured he'd been breathing on his own for a considerable time now. "Please," I thought, "Please don't let this be a new threat to his life."

Screwing up my courage and concentration, I focused all my attention on the Registrar.

"Let's check your drugs," he was saying – speaking directly to Charlie at last. Item by item he went through a long litany of pills and intravenous infusions to consider whether any of them could be responsible for the crisis, but nothing struck a chord with him, or with the entourage. He got to the end of the list and there was a silence... into which Charlie croaked:

"And Voltarol?"

"Voltarol?" echoed the Registrar. "Ilizeroff patients aren't prescribed Voltarol. There's a possibility it inhibits bone growth. Were you on it at the Infirmary?"

Charlie nodded: "And in ITU, and when I first came up here."

"Ah," said the Registrar.

Voltarol is an anti-inflammatory drug and Charlie had been on a high dosage. With its removal from his daily cocktail of medication, the tissue inside his chest cavity around his broken ribs had swollen unchecked. No wonder he was in difficulty.

A huge Voltarol suppository was instantly prescribed and brought to Charlie's bedside by one of the relieved and smiling ward nurses. Now a solution was in sight, I could see how worried the nursing staff had become and I felt a twinge of remorse at how fiercely assertive we'd been with them earlier. They might have waited longer than we'd have liked but they hadn't been taking the situation lightly by any means.

The nurse wielding the mega-suppository was about Charlie's own age; blonde, blue-eyed and drop-dead-gorgeous. Well he'd never have got the monster up his own bottom, so amidst a certain amount of painful laughter, he submitted to the inevitable indignity ... and afterwards, to his credit, he managed to look her in the eye and say thank you.

A mere twenty minutes later his breathing began to ease. By mid-evening he was OK. While the medics put their heads together about a Voltarol substitute, Charlie consumed his first, small, meal in twenty-four hours and the rest of us sat around his bed in a weary but warm cocoon of near-silence.

Since not much was said, it's not hard for me to remember and smile at the way Charlie turned to his brother at one point, and in a bloke-ish, offhand, "Thanks mate," kind of tone, the tone that young men feel comfortable with, managed to express a real and deep gratitude: "Whenever I looked," he said to Tim, "you were always *there*."

*

The scruffy diary recording this crisis tells me that two days later I accepted an invitation to supper at a restaurant with a friend. Peter was away on a business trip and I remember thinking that an evening with her would be a chance to talk - a relaxing and helpful distraction. In the event, the diary records:

'Supper. In retrospect, not really what I needed. Wanted a quiet tete-a-tete with friend but when I arrived, found she'd invited two others as well. Couldn't cope with the group. Could only talk about Charlie, but felt like 'the entertainment for the evening.' Stupid and ungrateful, I know. They meant well. I suppose they thought I needed taking out of myself. Afterwards phoned Sarah and she was lovely. Confirmed we all feel fragile and vulnerable.'

*

All change involves loss, and grief follows in the wake of loss just as night follows day. I think how even a wanted and planned-for change – a first baby, for instance – means saying goodbye to certain familiar and comfortable aspects of life – the freedom to go out in the evenings, the freedom to sleep all night, the freedom to be occasionally, wildly irresponsible. How much more difficult, then, is the gradual dawning that an unwanted and unpleasant upheaval in life is going to change everything, possibly for ever.

That's where we were right then. After the breakneck pace of Charlie's initial surgery there was, for him, a pause in which he could recover some strength. We, on the other hand, had been propelled and even sustained by the drama of events. Now in this pause we had time to reflect. And reflection was not easy.

At the very least, Charlie was going to suffer much pain and face the risk that it would all be in vain, for a considerable time. He would need a high level of physical care and a great deal of mental and emotional support. He would not be in a position to make the kind of life decisions his newly-graduated friends were taking, and he would inevitably feel useless and left behind. We, his parents, would look after him, but he wasn't a child. We would need to offer a different kind of care from anything we'd managed before.

Grief isn't only about loss. It's also about being burdened. In our case it was about the awful realisation that, having come through a situation that had tested us to our limits, the testing would go on and on – well into the foreseeable future.

A miracle is fantastic, but it doesn't make life easier. In fact, such an astonishing turn of events throws up endless difficulties, obvious, predictable ones and problems you never even imagined.

*

Saul of Tarsus, did he grieve, I wonder? After what happened on the Road to Damascus, I mean. He had plenty of time to reflect.

That's something I hadn't quite taken on board until now.

When you study Saul / St Paul, the story proceeds at a brisk pace. One minute he's a rising young star in the Pharisaic firmament, the next he's experiencing a life-shattering conversion en route to Damascus, and the next he's up and away on long and arduous missionary journeys to the Greco-Roman world of the Gentiles. But hang on, it didn't quite happen that way – neither according to *Acts* nor according to Paul's surviving letters. The man was no overnight success as a Christian. For the Jesus movement he wasn't, in reality, a great catch; in fact he clearly seemed more trouble than he was worth. In Damascus he was regarded with suspicion to say the least, and he failed to ride it out by keeping a low profile. To the first Christians, Saul of Tarsus was undoubtedly a liability – headstrong and difficult and dangerous – and for an appreciable period he was firmly side-lined. And, oh yes, he had plenty of time to ponder all that he'd lost.

The conversion of Saul on the Damascus road (*Acts 9:1-19*) is such a dramatic story, such a turning point in the known history of Christianity, that we can really not prevent ourselves from thinking about it in the light of what became of St Paul afterwards. It is almost impossible to comprehend the personal magnitude of what happened to Saul the Pharisee that day.

Luke describes it on three different occasions in *Acts*, relating slightly different though not mutually exclusive details each time, and each time, the breathtaking drama of the event is the staggering 'bolt from the blue' that stopped Saul in his tracks, turned him through 360 degrees and utterly changed his life. The man who set out for Damascus intending to persecute the followers of Jesus, arrived, blinded and staggering, intent on becoming one of their number.

The force of the story surely derives from the fact that we've all experienced this kind of thing, though hardly to this degree. I guess we've all had moments when 'the light dawns' on us and some fiendishly complicated issue we've been wrestling with, suddenly becomes crystal clear and simplicity itself. Moments when the way ahead is so 'blindingly obvious' we can't believe we haven't seen it all along. Moments that change our lives radically and for ever.

Of course, transforming one's life like this is hugely disruptive, and the chances are ten to one the new path won't be any smoother, straighter or one bit easier than the old. And if we think that our dramatic change of heart will bring us all the answers, that there'll be no more wrestling with complexities and our lives will be all sunshine – forget it.

Life is about growth and growth is mostly a struggle.

*

I bring to mind a 'Damascus event' of my own, which happened when I was sixteen. For a long time it seemed to me ironic, because it appeared to be the Saul story in reverse.

I grew up in a family where religion was respected and quite frequently discussed, but there was little or no pressure to practise. Nevertheless, I happily attended Sunday school as a child, and in my teens I used the scriptural knowledge rather haphazardly acquired, to continue studying at secondary level. It was A-level that brought things to a head.

For I had started the course with the assumption that A-level R.E. would broaden my understanding of religion and provide answers to the questions that were beginning to undermine my faith. Wrong.

It forced me to think deeply and to examine first principles – the first of all being the very existence of God. And to my dismay, I couldn't crack it. The bible I was now required to read intensively seemed little more than a collection of folk tales. Its solemn moral injunctions, just common-sense ethics and its belief in a magic being who somehow ran the show, juvenile.

So there I was, sitting on my bed one winter's night, looking up at the moon and the stars through the branches of a tree that grew outside my window. I was about to get up and draw the curtains but the night sky was so clear and beautiful, I hesitated. And in that moment it occurred to me that the vast, unimaginable universe, of which I could see such a tiny part, could not possibly be explained.

Religion was human, culturally determined and limited; the cosmos was of another order and the 'big' questions it provoked were unanswerable. Religion was man's response to ultimate uncertainty – fascinating to consider, scholarly even, but 'made-up' for all that. And God was pretend. I held this thought for quite a while, and the longer I sat with it, the more comfortable it felt. By the time I stirred myself to close the curtains, I had decided I was a Humanist, not a Christian. I had concluded that although religion was a perfectly valid subject for study, it was not a rational foundation for life. And thinking all this through I felt the burden of perplexity lift from my shoulders, while the relief of intellectual satisfaction filled my mind.

It did change my life. My God – the God of Sunday school and Scripture lessons – was shattered into a thousand pieces and could never be reconstituted. But while I firmly believed I had turned my back on the God-Question, the Question itself refused to reciprocate.

Over the next few years I sustained an amused and what I thought was an objective interest in comparative religion, and like many others of my generation I was intrigued by the spirituality of the East. I continued to respect and even envy my religious friends but I was pretty sure I would never again be one of them.

I'd better finish this reminiscence. The Question, to my irritation, hung around, mostly in the background … until I gave birth to my first child, a baby girl. Then, to my surprise, I realised that I was mothering on instinct. That despite my inexperience versus the experience of Health Visitors, the advice of friends and the well-thumbed pages of Dr Spock, my maternal instinct was quite astonishingly reliable.

So gradually I started, with great reluctance I might say, to examine my religious instincts too. And thus began a slow return to my Christian roots, shuffling back through a door that had never quite closed, to a new place – a bit on the edge of things - but back just inside a structure that could help me grow.

*

All of a sudden they announced they were preparing him for discharge. It shouldn't have come as a shock but it did. There was no more surgery planned for Charlie for a while and he'd been moved from an observation bed close to the nursing station to a bay at the end of the ward. He was doing well and, for the moment, he simply needed to get mentally and physically stronger. But to do this, he required more structure to his day, which was difficult for the nurses to provide on a busy ward, and real rest at night, which was hard when the confused old man opposite screamed and struggled out of bed. We could see clearly that hospital was now beginning to hamper Charlie's progress. But it seemed unthinkable that we could manage at home.

The truth was, we'd become hospital-dependent. We felt safe, even comfortable, in the institutionalised, seen-it-all-before confidence of the place. The staff who never flapped, the 24/7 help on hand, even the predictable hassles with car parking and the occasional 'grumpy day' with Charlie.

We were coping, and for the first time in weeks, our anxiety levels were pretty much parentally normal. Now, all this massive, expensive support that had held us tight through the crisis was going to be withdrawn – of course it was - but how on earth would we cope? Scarcely had the news sunk in than a discharge date was set and wheels went into motion at a dizzying pace.

With all the activity, it was impossible to dwell on potential difficulties, so we didn't. Physiotherapy gave Charlie a blistering exercise regime. Nursing gave him tests on the care of his Ilizeroff frame. Occupational Therapy gave him gadgets: perching stools, grabbing sticks and best of all, a shiny new wheelchair.

The moment it arrived on the ward, we got Charlie into it and I pushed him wherever he commanded. Through the double doors of Trauma we went and out into the vast warren of the hospital. Charlie was thrilled. We had lunch in the restaurant, bought a newspaper and some chocolate at the newsagent's and spent time browsing amongst the medical books in Blackwell's.

As I wheeled him back to the ward, an exhausted but 'mobile' Charlie declared: "I couldn't be more pleased if I'd been given a Porsche!"

We were on top of the world – a world that, for Charlie, now extended beyond his bed.

And so the discharge date grew closer. It *was* going to be wonderful to have him at home! On the other hand, as every new day arrived, I began to watch with ferocious concentration and no little apprehension as the calm, efficient nurses managed Charlie's complicated daily routine. Oh my! Very soon, all this care would be down to me ... clumsy, absent-minded me.

*

As my diary instantly has me recalling those feelings of anxiety about how would I cope with my new responsibility I find I've got to a place in *Acts (9:20-30)* where Saul must have grappled with new responsibility too.

And I wonder whether he ever considered keeping a low profile in Damascus? To quietly join the Jesus movement and listen and learn? Probably not. He was committed and impetuous and, I guess, imbued with all the confidence and certainty of youth.

But his forceful preaching in public places was not wise. Quite soon it seems that some in the Jewish community plotted to kill this turncoat. And Paul himself suggests (in *2 Corinthians 11*) that the Damascus Christians were rather keen to get shot of their dangerous new convert. They didn't want him to die but neither did they want to be party to such trouble that they themselves might die, and so they engineered his escape. At night, lowered in a basket from a house on the city walls. An undignified exit.

And where did Saul go? From one of his letters (*Galatians 1*) it seems he visited Arabia for a time, perhaps quite a long time, before making his way back to Jerusalem … where Luke relates how he was cold-shouldered by the Christians there.

Eventually it seems he was befriended by Barnabus, who spoke up for Saul, telling the apostles how he had risked his life for the cause. As a result, he got to meet Peter and James and was given a remit to work with the Greek-speaking Jews in the city. Unfortunately, no sooner had he begun, than his fervent preaching re-ignited trouble for the movement. So once again, Saul was hustled away, first to Caesarea and before long, home to Tarsus. And there he remained, out of serious contact with the Christians in Jerusalem, out of the limelight, out of the picture. The early history of Christianity proceeded without him – and got on very well.

He must have had moments of grief, back in Tarsus, I'm sure. Not necessarily regret, but dreadful pangs of loss as he thought about his high-flying promise as a young man. Of how he'd excelled in his studies of the law – perhaps at the feet of the eminent Rabbi

Gamaliel himself. Of how he, with his considerable energy, had been noticed and entrusted with the responsibility of opposing the Jesus movement. And of how he, a Jew of the tribe of Benjamin, a scholar and a Roman citizen had been ostracised by those charismatic Galilean fishermen he now so badly wanted to serve. There was much to mourn, indeed in later life he was not above mentioning all he had lost in becoming a Christian (*Philippians* 3) and I guess that for him to have stayed in Tarsus and remained loyal must have entailed much eating of humble pie by this complex and difficult man.

I have to remind myself that Saul wouldn't have known that he wasn't destined to end his days in obedient obscurity in Tarsus – and yet he remained. That says a lot, I think.

*

I call the diary 'scruffy' because it consists of two very ordinary, unprepossessing notebooks, but though they're a bit thumbed, they're not in bad condition, after all, the diary was something to *write* not to read.

When I do flick through it, I'm uncomfortably transported back in time. Many of the entries are terse, yet conjuring up this or that situation with poignant accuracy:

Discharged Home! Great stuff! Only thing – he seemed so agile and capable in hospital and so fit in comparison to some of the other patients. At home the full extent of his incapacity is evident – and how far he has still to go.

I should say so.

That morning, the paramedics carried Charlie up three flights of stairs to his own small bedroom at the top of the house. This is where he wanted to be, back in his own space, and the grin on his face as they propped him up on his own bed made the effort worthwhile. For the manhandling involved in the whole business of transporting him from hospital ward to home bedroom caused him considerable pain. The paramedics were as gentle and kind as they could be, but when they left, Charlie swallowed a large handful of pain-killers to counteract the throbbing in the pin-sites of his Ilizeroff frame, the soreness of the long scar on his abdomen and the stinging discomfort of his skin grafts.

Then we just sat, and drank tea together in calm, comfortable silence. Peter came home for a while at lunchtime to celebrate, and the three of us shared a picnic of all the odd little food treats Charlie had missed in hospital. Peaceful and happy, we savoured those precious moments, living entirely in the present.

Later that afternoon Charlie and I tackled our first practical test. The next door bathroom was no great distance away but we had only a sketchy idea of how he might get there for the morning bath that was a crucial part of his Ilizeroff routine. So we decided to practise our strategy – without doing the bath bit. It was dire.

He had a little strength in his right arm, which had a longitudinal metal pin in it, and some use of his left leg. He could also stand briefly, when he was balanced, the frame on his right leg supporting his weight. To help us, we had a perching stool so he could rest at every step without having to actually sit down.

I remember wishing Peter hadn't gone back to work. As it was, Charlie and I struggled. Just getting himself started involved a slow inching to the edge of the bed, followed by a rocking movement and a kind of timed bear-hug by me to haul him to his feet. This, followed by collapse on to the perching stool. Then, after getting his breath back, we set off for the bathroom. Stand up, step forward with left foot, bring right leg alongside, advance stool one pace, collapse on it again. Repeat.

Five minutes, and we still hadn't reached the bedroom door; this was clearly going to take ages. Five turned to ten and then twenty minutes. As we finally made it beyond the door, there was nothing for it but to laugh. That or cry. Our laughter had an edge of hysteria to it but was therapeutic nonetheless. Then off again.

The journey to the bathroom was epic – and its achievement was celebrated with cheering and a pee. Returning was definitely faster – our technique was improving – until Charlie regained his bed with a partially-controlled fall. No damage, thank goodness. Triumph! He sighed with relief and carefully stretched himself out.

And then quite suddenly, he slept; grey-faced with exhaustion, leaning awkwardly on pillows that had somehow slipped sideways.

I'd looked away for a moment and Charlie had abandoned himself to sleep... and I was lonely as he slept.

*

I ponder change. Mostly it comes gradually. We grow up, develop personal relationships, build careers, start families, plan change then implement it. Most of this kind of change involves a gradual letting-go of some elements of our way of life in order to develop others. But every so often fate throws a thunderbolt at us and a change we'd never have desired or contemplated is thrust upon us. And that hurts. We lose our job, or our health, or a loved one, and we scrabble to adjust to the new reality of our lives.

Or something huge and extraordinary, like a miracle, happens. And, oh yes, a miracle is an amazing joy and an incredible blessing – but our lives are rent asunder just the same, and there is loss. The event, be it catastrophic or miraculous (and of course we'd all fervently pray for the latter) divides our life in the same way into 'before' and 'after', 'then' and 'now'. Somehow, if we're to maintain mental balance and a coherent sense of our own identity, we have to repair and renew the threads of life that have been severed out of the blue.

Work-related reading in the field of social science reminds me of a metaphor used by the scholar Peter Marris, though he doubtless wasn't its originator. Anyway, he describes one's life as being like a tapestry, woven by the individual as he or she lives and grows and develops. An unexpected, traumatic event is experienced, he says, as though someone has taken a huge pair of scissors to the tapestry and cut it from top to bottom. The weaver is distraught. The emerging pattern, so long in the making, is ruined. The tapestry has to continue, but despite the weaver's desperate efforts to keep going, it now looks disordered and different and wrong. At some point the weaver has to stop and return to the rent in the fabric, and make it good – join the new and the old together and devise a more complex, and perhaps more beautiful, whole. The process must begin with an unflinching look at the old material: the past, the lost. And there is no serious loss without grief and grieving.

*

In my mind I'm back at Charlie's bedside that first day he was home from hospital. My beautiful son, sleeping. No longer healthy and strong, no more the carefree young student, but pale, scarred and exhausted. The boy with the floppy blonde hair who captained the struggling cricket team, the confident teenager who place-kicked for his rugby side, the young adult who was planning to run the marathon in a rhino suit for charity – all past tense.

He'll never again play in a football team, never, on a summer's afternoon, dive for a catch on the boundary, never again run like the wind. Instead, he will suffer indignity and pain. He will lose freedom and choice, and he will be dependent on other people for a long time to come. It is a miracle that he lives, but the pattern of his life – and our lives –from now on will be changed.

It's a relief to get back to *Acts*, though I don't lose the theme of miracles, so I'm not exactly 'off the hook'. But I'm thinking that if the Luke who compiled *Luke – Acts* was indeed a physician, it's not altogether surprising he was big on the miraculous, being a professional healer himself and therefore interested in such things.

Two thousand years later, however, it doesn't play so well.

Thinking about it, it's not that we don't like miracles any more. Far from it. We comb the news for the occasional bright star of an 'against all the odds' story. The old lady pulled alive from the rubble of an earthquake when all around is death and destruction. The child who lives and whose health improves despite the doctors' decision not to resuscitate. The release of a hostage. The bloodless revolution. These things give us hope and make us glad.

Miracles do happen and we, as frail human beings, prone to despondency and quick to quit when things get tough, need the odd miracle. Even today.

It's miracle *workers* we don't like these days. We expect our physicists, chemists, biologists and doctors to explain exactly how their tricks work, and mostly, they can. Even when they can't, though, they'll have a stab at an explanation, give a hypothesis.. For we insist that everything is ultimately explicable to us, rationally, logically and demonstrably so. Magicians are for children, psychics impress only the gullible, and faith-healers are deluded, we say. We are highly sceptical and deeply distrust anyone who seems to make inexplicable things happen – and rightly so. But do we go too far? Does our obsession with factual explanation become a limit to our growth? I suspect it does. Well, it does for me.

*

I'm musing on this because I've arrived at a section in *Acts* that focuses on Peter (*Acts 9: 31-43, 12:1-23*)

As with Jesus, so with Peter. Everywhere he went he seems to have brought excitement, hope and healing. He must have been an extraordinary person to know. Proof positive in Peter's case that you don't have to be perfect yourself to bring help and love to others. Peter who denied Jesus thrice, who ran away and was not there at the crucifixion. Peter who worried desperately about the way the message of Jesus was spreading beyond the horizons of his own world. Peter, with all his human fallibilities, who did not always understand but was nevertheless possessed of such warmth and sincere concern that amazing things happened around him.

In Lydda, a paralysed man called Aeneas stood up and walked. In Joppa, a well-loved woman called Tabitha fell sick and apparently died, but when Peter came to pray by her bedside, she opened her eyes and lived again. Luke recounts such healing events almost in passing. I have no 'explanation' to offer, and I cannot help wondering what happened to these people *afterwards.*

Then there's an angel! My word! Angels to me have about the same status as ghosts. I've never seen either and I don't expect to. But don't get me wrong, I'm not dismissing the phenomena as illusory. It's more that I can't quite fathom in what sense they're to be understood. In any case, I'm very fond of angel stories, allied as they usually are with good news and miracles.

Anyway, the story goes that around this time, the Jesus movement attracted the antipathy of King Herod – and now it was the Aramaic-speaking Christians in Jerusalem who were targeted. We're told that James, the brother of John, was arrested and beheaded.

This accomplished, Herod moved against Peter, who was taken and held while arrangements were made for a show trial. But it was not his time to die.

We have this wonderful story of how, on the night before his trial he was awoken by an angel, whose presence filled his cell with light. The chains that secured him between two guards fell away and the angel impatiently urged him to put on his cloak and follow him out. In a daze he did so, thinking dimly that it was some kind of dream. They passed first one guard post then another until they reached the iron gate to the prison – which opened of its own accord. Then down the length of a street Peter walked with the angel.

It wasn't until the angel quietly left him that Peter came to his senses and realised he was at liberty in Jerusalem in the middle of the night and that he'd better quickly seek refuge or he'd be re-captured.

So hurrying through the sleeping city, he reached the house of Mary, mother of John Mark, and knocked insistently at the door. A stunned housemaid called Rhoda recognised his low, urgent voice and in her confusion she left him standing outside, still knocking, while she went to blurt out the news to the rest of the household. They thought she was completely crazy! Finally, she was accompanied to the door where Peter stood, large as life, signalling for them to be quiet. So he escaped.

It's a powerful story. The plum prisoner eludes Herod's grasp. Instead, it's Herod himself for whom time is running out, and shortly afterwards, it is he who dies. Meanwhile, Peter and the growing brotherhood of Christians, continue to flourish.

*

I ask myself how I should interpret the story. There are strong intimations of the operation of Fate here – or maybe it would be more biblically correct to call it the working out of a divine plan.

Peter is rescued; he has much more work to do, while the arrogant King Herod is finally condemned. And that's all rather satisfying.

Only, I can't be doing with Fate. I believe in free will. In man's ability to choose and in choosing, to influence his own destiny.

The fate thing – what sometimes appears to be an inexorable tide of events that carries us along, whether we like it or not – is, I think, the result of our being or not being 'on the beam' … on the right path for us.

When we're on the beam, we find it possible to achieve a kind of harmony in our lives that promotes understanding, kindness and aims we can be proud of. When we're off it, life becomes an uphill struggle and the temptation to cheat or hurt to achieve our wayward goals, grows ever stronger. Not Fate, I think, but awareness and free choice.

Life is never going to be easy, but choose well and it will be rich and satisfying.

So how many of us choose well, every time …? For most of us, I guess, whole chunks of our life can seem like one gigantic wobble after another.

*

Next day Charlie tried doing stairs, shuffling along on his bottom, using his arms and the strength of his left leg to propel himself from one stair to another – slow work but just about possible. It was another important manoeuvre, since we'd have to take him from home to outpatient appointments, and they were due to begin quite soon. The skill of stairs, though, had immediate rewards for it meant that, albeit with considerable effort, he could choose to be in surroundings other than his bedroom. Charlie's small, cosy room at the top of the house that was his sanctuary on Day 1, could, we were all too aware, become a prison.

And, of course it wasn't long before the worry became a reality:

'Yesterday, after rather a lot of stairs, Charlie's pin-sites were sore. Today it's clear he has a fully-fledged infection in his leg. Called GP and he's

back on antibiotics with leg elevated. ...'

'It's not surprising Charlie feels miserable. Confined to his room, he can't see the point of getting up, washing or shaving. But the routine, with physio, is crucial to maintaining a structure and purpose to our day.

'I hate nagging, but whatever I do - gentle persuasion or businesslike negotiation - it comes across that way. Sometimes he will move, sometimes he won't. I can't always find a way to help him and I so wish I could do more. Helplessness is awful.'

But then, the following day:

'Another hard day with hurting pin-sites – but a moving conversation with Charlie about what he could remember from the early part of his time in hospital – when his life still hung in the balance. He thought for a bit and then said that his first memory was of a relieved awareness that he could breathe and he could think. He knew something immense had happened but he wasn't scared.

He also said that he was aware from very early on when people were trying to communicate with him, and he knew how much everybody cared. This was wonderful, but irritating at times - placing on him a felt obligation to respond to us all, even when he longed to simply drift ...'

*

Obligation is a difficult one.

'At Caesarea there was a man named Cornelius, a centurion in the Italian cohort.' (Acts 10:1-48).

Jesus was a Jew. A Jew who worshipped at the Temple, however much he criticised it, and revered the Torah, even if he did have harsh words for those who observed its letter whilst flouting its spirit. Peter was a Jew too, and he cared about the health of Judaism. But there was a problem.

The teachings of Jesus from within that faith were inspirational, and they had struck a chord with many Jews. The gospel now being spread by Peter and his friends was certainly Jewish, but it was Jewish-with-a-difference. For it was spiritually inclusive – broad enough and deep enough and startlingly clear – so that anyone at all who was interested could begin in their own way, to follow its precepts. And, to the consternation of Peter, this was coming to include not only hereditary Jews – with their reassuring grounding in the scriptures and acceptance of dietary laws and social customs, but a few Gentile God-fearers as well. What to do with them? What, if anything, could Gentiles be given? And if given something, what should be demanded of them in return?

*

In twenty-first century terms, I guess there's an organisational parallel that can be drawn with commercial expansion in the market place, and the danger – no, certainty – of dilution that goes with it. The smart little company with innovative ideas, a busy, purposeful ethos and an egalitarian workforce that succeeds ... and expands ... and starts to operate like a bigger company ... with procedures and rules and managers, and a telephone customer service department that plays a recorded message. With cost-cutting and consumer-profiling so that the company grows some more ... until it looks like any other big business, and is every bit as soulless. We can all think of enterprises that have remorselessly gone this way: the little firms who forget their roots, neglect their core customers and opt for growth at any price.

So I have a lot of sympathy with Peter. Growth at any price could never be acceptable for the followers of Jesus. But he went for growth in the end though. Because faith isn't a commodity to be purchased, to be offered or withheld as the vendor pleases. It's a treasure to be sought. And guides have a primary obligation to assist, not to judge.

Peter's decision-making didn't come easily – witness his troubled dream with its upsetting command to eat meat forbidden to Jews. Witness his carefully thought-out justification to his brethren after teaching and baptising the whole household of the Roman centurion, Cornelius. But he had seen for himself how Gentiles could be filled with the Holy Spirit, just like Jews, and his curious dream had confirmed his understanding that the entirety of creation was sacred – that no living creature should be described as 'unclean'.

And so, it seems the inclusion of some Gentiles amongst the Christian brotherhood was accepted in principle. If Peter believed this was allowable, then the others would not deny it. But it was huge, really. In practice, it threw up all manner of further questions that I know I'll be coming to later. Like: should the apostles now make a point of taking the teachings of Jesus to Gentiles who might be receptive? And: if a Gentile wanted to join the movement, should he be obliged to publicly demonstrate his respect for the Law by which Jesus himself had lived? Questions that would continue to plague Peter, and would divide the early church for years to come.

*

Charlie's first outpatient appointment. JR Hospital 2.00pm. Light lunch, early, in order to painstakingly load as follows:

Lift wheelchair from folded position by front door and unfold (it's an unwieldy, uncooperative beast). Help Charlie into chair, manhandle it over threshold and down ramp to front path, thence to car. Help Charlie from chair to car. Rush back to collect appointment card and set phone to answer machine mode. Re-fold chair (uncooperative beast) and heave

*it into boot. (Heavy as well). Did I lock front door? Back to check. Drive
to hospital. Find parking space and pay for it with right money (hoarded
in advance). Unloading: well, procedure in reverse – and a dash to clinic,
arriving just on time – but to find that all patients had similar appointments for 2.00pm. Long wait in prospect now, but in fact an opportunity
to recover breath and soothe frazzled nerves.*

To be honest, it's quite nice to be back.

Having brought the diary with me in case we needed facts and
dates recorded in its pages, I'd cheerfully scribbled the above, but
the day's entry stops there. I wrote up the ensuing appointment
briefly, later.

The Consultant, Martin McNally, was pleased with Charlie's
overall health, but recurrent infections had made his leg too
painful to bear his weight for very long. As a result, McNally said,
bone growth was a bit disappointing. Though he smiled a lot, and
his tone was nothing if not positive, we could see from today's X-
ray that bone growth was in fact infinitesimal:

Oh, God, not all this for nothing?

Gently, McNally admitted this sometimes happened and said not
to worry, he'd keep an eye on things. In the meantime, we were to
be sent off to Physiotherapy to get a foot pump. This, Charlie was
to use to provide exercise resistance on days when he couldn't
stand. The appointment came to an end and Charlie shook hands
and grinned and went along with everyone's 'chin up' heartiness,
but afterwards, at home, he was pole-axed.

How do you put a positive slant on news like this?

I close the scruffy diary firmly and put it away. It still has the
power to bring me to tears.

Acts once again is a relief, and instead of reading a new passage, I drop back into more thinking about issues of 'belonging' to a faith community. For the apostles, letting the odd Gentile God-fearer into membership of the Jesus movement was all very well, but if they chose not to adopt the outward symbols and practices of the Judaism that Jesus and his followers embraced, how then would their membership be demonstrated?

Of course, I know the answer that gradually came to be accepted – membership was proclaimed through baptism, participation in the eucharist and adherence to an emerging system of beliefs about Jesus as Christ.

And here's an oddity. Alone of all the great religions, the practice of Christianity is structured less around actions and more around beliefs. Christians can and do participate in a wide range of ceremonies and customs – or none – and still call themselves Christians... provided, that is, they can assent in some fashion to the creeds of the Church. Yes, I'm aware there are historical and political explanations for this state of affairs but it still seems odd to me. For 'belief' in reality isn't nearly as straightforward or as unifying as it sounds.

I bet that each and every one of us who call ourselves Christians has come to a point over some issue of belief where 'towing the party line' has proved difficult. Not least because if you search hard enough you can find almost as many 'party lines' as there are Christians. The mainstream of opinion has shifted over time and continues to shift, while heresies come and go under different names, exploring aspects of the fringe.

Sure, all the followers of world religions have beliefs – and all encompass within them a spectrum of linked ideas. But Christianity continues to be obsessed by belief, in a way that I think would have been quite foreign to Jesus.

It's a real problem, since in my view Christianity persists because it's vibrant and challenging and it works, not because a collection of people can agree on a list of things they all believe.

Religion isn't really about giving intellectual assent to things that other people proclaim to be true, it's about awareness of a spiritual dimension to existence. It's about the way this awareness affects the life you lead, with others and for others. And it's about shaping this life through our fleeting experiences of the divine. As a Christian I recite the Creed and I think it's beautiful, but actually a bit of a farce. I'm certainly not alone in needing to execute some mental gymnastics as I declaim, believing one thing literally and another symbolically or metaphorically – for who can say for sure what the words actually mean? 'I believe in God' can mean one thing to you and another to me. How likely is it that our concepts of the Unimaginable will be the same? And after that, the Creed just gets more difficult.

I have a friend who finds the whole idea of the Holy Spirit ungraspable. Me? I can do Holy Spirit; I like Spirit. It's the 'only begotten Son' bit I wrestle with. You see, the belief that Jesus Christ was fully human, is kind of spoilt for me by the insistence not just that he is the Son of God – so might you or I be – but he is the *only* Son of God. Well, that makes Jesus a very different sort of creature from you or me. But that's my problem. I give it an airing now and again. We're encouraged to worship *with all our mind*, and I hope my fellow Christians can treat my difficulty with respectful gentleness.

*

At last it had all started to improve. A window of opportunity without pin-site infections had got Charlie up on his feet, bearing his weight, so that his fibula and tibia bones had begun to grow. Still not much, but at least they were off the starting blocks.

He was given crutches, and they were absolutely brilliant! Suddenly he was able to move around the house in an easy, upright position instead of his previous best-practice of getting across the floor in a slow, crab-like crawl.

*

Melissa's mother visited one day, bearing a huge potted hydrangea plant and some cheerful news: Melissa was returning from Italy, to be based for a while in London. Charlie was pleased, more pleased than he cared to let on, even to himself, I think. He didn't, daren't think in terms of a serious relationship with her, but Melissa's friendship and her company were precious nonetheless.

I took a language student for ten days. Not someone new to me, but the son of an Italian diplomat that I'd taught before. Luca was now sixteen, an advanced student of English, wanting to hone his skills in preparation for international exams. Using a total immersion approach meant having the student live with us, and this was difficult given Charlie's regime, but Luca was considerate and flexible.

On the Day of the Setback I had taught a rather good morning's-worth on the subject of rhetoric. We'd dissected the eulogy delivered by Earl Spencer at the funeral of his sister, Princess Diana. With the aid of a newspaper transcript, plus video footage of the occasion, a potentially dry topic was transformed into something modern, moving and relevant. I was feeling pretty smug, and after supper, was boasting to Charlie about it. He'd stretched himself out on the sitting room sofa and was waiting happily for Melissa to arrive for the evening. All he did was to adjust his position on the sofa, but "Aaah!" he yelled.

"What?" I asked, alarmed.

"My arm," he groaned, "something's broken."

It was his right arm, the one with the long metal pin in it. He'd felt something snap and was in pain every time he moved. So Melissa arrived, not to a warm, cosy welcome but amidst preparations to get Charlie up to A & E. Peter was away on business, worse luck, so leaving Luca at home on his own, Charlie, Melissa and I set off for the hospital.

It was mid-evening when we arrived in A & E and the department was crowded and busy. Charlie in his wheelchair was rather aggressively cross-questioned by a harassed triage nurse, who wasn't inclined to believe that levering himself up to shift his position on a sofa was likely to cause either a bone or a metal rod to fracture. She examined him, hurt him – and he let rip. Not shouting, but with just-about-controlled lucidity, he protested vehemently at her hostility and demanded to be seen by someone else.

The nurse rapidly withdrew and we were left to stew for what seemed like a considerable time. Just as well, really, because it took the heat out of the situation. I went off to buy hot drinks from a vending machine while Charlie caught up with Melissa's news and gossip from the outside world. Soon, we were laughing, and that's how a distinctly apprehensive young doctor found us some time later.

Charlie's notes had, in the meantime, been located and the medical part of the evening re-started, this time in friendlier fashion. We were there virtually all night. An X-ray confirmed that the metal rod had indeed snapped and his arm was firmly strapped to immobilise it. Then we were sent home.

It hadn't been quite the evening Charlie and Melissa had planned but it was, to say the least, memorable.

Next morning, Luca's English was postponed, as Charlie and I went, bleary-eyed, back to the hospital to see McNally. Much hmm-ing and ha-ing over the X rays and eventually a decision. His arm was to be encased in a rigid brace and allowed to heal naturally. It would take time, but there'd be more X-rays in three to four weeks to ascertain progress.

Loads of reassurance, no major damage done, arm would be just fine. But it wasn't only, or even mainly, the arm. The fantastic, the wonderful crutches, just 'in,' were now 'out'. It was back to crawling for Charlie – that or his wheelchair – for weeks ... months? For the foreseeable future, anyway. And to set it off nicely, McNally deemed it necessary to return him to hospital for a three hour operation to adjust the Ilizeroff frame on his leg. Brilliant, eh?

*

Friends were a godsend – Charlie's and mine. Peter's too, for he also found the going heavy. I wasn't the best wife or the easiest person to live with at that time. I was so sure I *knew* how Charlie should be supported and threw myself into the task with every once of my energy.

Having been a Medical Social Worker for seven years in the past, I'd seen patients become bitter and defeated by disease or disability and I was determined this was *not* going to happen to Charlie. He needed love, care, optimism and as much independence as he could manage. And for the time being, he also needed to talk as often as he wanted, about whatever he wanted, for as long as he wanted. These were my priorities and I was convinced from the beginning that given these things, Charlie would not carry debilitating mental scars from the accident. Fighting talk, but still he had to heal – not only physically but also from shock and trauma, pain and loss.

I was pre-occupied with my son. Meanwhile my brave, unflappable, hard-working husband was shifting emotionally for himself. I did want to be there for everyone.

At one point I wrote with anguish: *'We MUST make good things come out of all this.'* But it was Peter who was neglected, and he undoubtedly felt it keenly. I was amassing a debt, an increasingly pressing need for some fence-mending to be done in our relationship.

* * *

BALANCE

Regaining balance after a period of turmoil is, I think, about re-assessing values. It's about finding again a point of stability, an inner certainty, and building upon that anew. Not aiming at a perfect life, tranquil harmony and all that – that isn't really life at all – but a balanced existence where see-sawing events and our off-the-wall reactions to them can be put in perspective in times of peaceful reflection. Once we have a stable point of balance to which we can return, life's inevitable difficulties deflect and discourage us less. We know pretty much what we wish for and where we're heading; we're aware of the core values that are pushing us in that direction and we grow in confidence that we can weather a few storms along the way.

But first, we have to find it, the stable point. Find it and test it out. It will not be the same as it was before the upheaval – things will never be the same – but it may give a truer, stronger, more mature focus for living. For I'm convinced of one thing: trying to recover the old balance isn't an option. It's tempting to be sure, but it leads only to nostalgia, or worse, to endless melancholy, and regret over outdated dreams. Renewed life – life after a miracle – requires a courageous staggering forward towards a new balance-point.

*

I look at a photo of Charlie. In a white tuxedo, re-tailored to accommodate the brace on his arm, standing by the car, about to go to a wedding. His wheelchair is being loaded into the boot and Melissa is waiting for him to accompany her to the marriage of her sister.

Charlie has taken ages to get ready – his entire getting-up routine now being awkwardly executed left-handedly – but he looks great. If you discount the strained expression on his face. His lips are smiling but his brow is furrowed with pain. Looking back, I know he's going to take some more pills and plunge into the wedding celebrations with all the energy he can muster. He will overcome his embarrassment at being chair-bound. He will accept the fuss and play the hero. He will not feel normal but he *will* feel wanted and happy. Melissa's Granny will throw her arms around him and hover protectively at his side. Guests will thoughtfully gather around his chair and ensure he's included in the conversation. By the end of the day Charlie will be both elated and exhausted, and after all this, two sets of parents will be both proud and worried.

It was quite a while before I truly appreciated the situation of Melissa's parents. So wrapped up was I in our own difficulties that I never stopped to think how anxious they might be. I'd welcomed Melissa's reappearance in Charlie's life unreservedly because she made him – and all of us – happy. Happy and whole and ordinary. With us, his Mum and Dad, the harsh truth for Charlie was that he'd reverted to being a dependent son. But with Melissa he was a brave and smiling young man who was already rebuilding his life. It was so good for him to get away from home and his parents every so often and stay at Melissa's house. Here, he was unfailingly treated with grown-up respect and could imagine he was independent.

But I never thought of these visits from Melissa's parents' point of view. Their beautiful, talented daughter was forming an ever more serious bond with a youth whose future was, to say the least, uncertain. Their relationship had flourished then diminished once before, so was there really more to it now, than need on his part and compassion on hers?

And, of course, there was the responsibility of having this unsteady invalid around the house and garden, prone as he was when standing, to attempt a few paces and proceed to totter and fall in a clatter of metal. As scary, really, as looking after someone else's toddler.

By this time, Peter and I, too, had our worries. We never doubted Melissa would remain a true friend to Charlie but what if she decided that friendship was as far as it went? Right now, Charlie adored her and was obviously entertaining thoughts that they might once again become 'an item'. It was a massive motivator to keep him going and stay positive, but we could hardly bear to think of the consequences of disappointment. We were afraid lest Charlie should be nurturing false hopes. Afraid he would fall hopelessly in love – but what could we do? It was happening anyway.

*

Worry. It focuses the mind marvellously.

I'm off again on my journey through *Acts* and I surmise (from 11: 9-30) that the church in Jerusalem was worried about Antioch. Anyway, it ended up taking some momentous decisions that were eventually to shift the balance of the Jesus movement for ever. But first, a trusted envoy, Barnabus, was dispatched to investigate.

Antioch in Syria was big. It had a flourishing Jewish community and a vigorous, growing band of Christians. In fact Antioch is apparently where the followers of Jesus were first called 'Christians'. And it was here that the movement first attracted a sizeable number of Gentiles. For the mother church in Jerusalem, this must have been an anxiety. I imagine the discussions that would have gone on, late into the night at the house of Mary, John Mark's mother, and elsewhere. Until now, newcomers to the movement had been limited to Jews or Gentile proselytes - 'God-fearers.' But if things went as they seemed to be going in Antioch, there could in future be congregations of believers where pagan converts were in the majority. Was this to be feared or embraced?

Barnabus, *Acts* says, was a *good* man, and I have to admit to a bit of a soft spot for him. For one thing, he came from Cyprus – an enchantingly beautiful island with a fascinating history. For another, he seems to have possessed a generosity of spirit and an open-minded approach to problems that brought out the best in people. So off he went to Antioch and he was seriously impressed by what he found. A mixed, Greek-speaking community of Jews, proselytes and pagans, working together and seeking teaching and guidance in the Christian Way. He obviously reassured the Jerusalem brethren that this community in Antioch was a healthy organisation in an exciting entrepot city, from whence the word could easily spread even further. He was going to stay and help them get on their feet. There's no indication of dissenting voices from Jerusalem: that the church in Antioch was the real thing, seems to have been accepted.

To my mind, this positive acceptance of the mixed Antioch congregation marks the beginning of a search for a new point of balance for the expanding Jesus movement. I think in retrospect, this step, authorised by spiritual Jews, towards including those whose religious grounding was in the pagan philosophies of the wider Greco-Roman world, was definitive. It opened the door to a potent blend of thought-patterns. A blend that would eventually forge a new Christian identity that would resonate throughout the western world.

Barnabus took that step and took it with confidence at the time. Perhaps he regretted it later, when the balance really did begin to swing. But there and then, having decided the good Christians of Antioch needed support, he journeyed to Tarsus to seek out his energetic colleague, Saul. A persuasive man, it wasn't long before he'd co-opted Saul to return with him to Antioch. Knowing how the story goes, I think he possibly regretted his choice of Saul too, further down the line.

*

We're already half way through Lent and the shops are full of Mother's Day cards: arty, pretty, funny, sentimental, expensive, but essentially *untruthful* about motherhood. Not that I'd opt out – I enjoy the business of choosing a card and buying flowers or a small gift for my elderly Mum, and she enjoys being on the receiving end. As do I, I have to admit. But, honestly, they're a bit wide of the mark aren't they? All those images of straw hats and picnics, of cute children or bright flowers or dizzy cartoon mums drinking champagne.

Motherhood is a sight more basic than that. It's about being heavily pregnant at the most inconvenient of times, and usually when the weather has turned suffocatingly hot and your ankles swell up – or maybe freezing cold when none of your coats meet in the middle to fasten. It's about long or painful labours, when you're too tired to do the breathing properly and you feel anything but in control. It's about the joy of a newborn infant but it's also about the immensity of the responsibility you now assume for the wellbeing of this little scrap, when you scarcely know how to keep going yourself. It's about sleepless nights – years and years of them, actually – and days of worry or guilt when things go wrong. As they inevitably do.

Children remain your children even when they've reached adulthood and know a great deal more about the ways of the world than you do. And whilst you may not be able to help or even influence your grown-up children very much, motherhood continues to evoke a deep, protective, visceral response towards them always – for the rest of your life. Show me a card that says all that!

*

Clinic. Excellent. Leg doing well. Arm: 60% chance of healing without intervention. Physio will concentrate on his neck, which is painful. Consultant suggested a couple of sessions of counselling to give Charlie an opportunity to vent some of his anger and frustration.

I smile wryly to myself on reading about the counselling. An appointment came through ten months later – far too late. By then, Charlie found it amusing. He politely declined to attend, saying that as he hadn't actually swung a baseball bat at anyone or taken to drink, he reckoned he was over the worst. As he was. But back then, things were hard.

Another entry reads:

Charlie very dispirited. Difficult to handle. I'm trying not to react too much to some of his barbed comments because I don't want him to feel he has to protect me. I think he must feel safe with me. He needs me to be an anchor – someone he can say whatever he likes to, in the knowledge that he won't pull me into the mire of anger / frustration / despair with him. It's hard sometimes and I'm using this diary to moan to!

*

Charlie was still some way from finding a new point of balance. Reading *Acts*, though, it strikes me that Antioch is maybe where Saul did it. In helping Barnabus for a whole year, Saul – this man with the most thoroughly Jewish of mind-sets - seems to have understood that his life's work henceforth was to go resolutely into the world of the Gentiles.

And I'm inclined to think that the extraordinary balance he achieved in his thinking and teaching, a balance between real respect and love for his converts from pagan cults and his continuing reverence for the Hebrew learning and scripture that was the heritage of Christians too, was cultivated there in Antioch and remained for the rest of his life.

It was in Antioch that the vibrant, mixed community of Christians took a decision to send Saul and Barnabus, together with the young man from Jerusalem called John Mark, onward into Cyprus, where there was a nucleus of brethren to whom Barnabus was known. Saul clearly jumped at the idea, and it was at about this time – at the start of his missionary journeying - that Saul became known as Paul. *(Acts 13:9)*

*

A name is so important. I think it's a surprisingly powerful springboard for our identity and *our* name is a label we hope will flatter us. As best we can, we kind-of grow into our names and then stretch them and adjust them to fit as we travel through life. But we don't have much to work on, for names are nearly always *given*. OK, the Pope gets to choose, and some entrants to religious orders, but for most of us, it's other folk who choose our names.

We're born and our parents hand on to us a family name. And then they select one or more personal names that seem good to them at the time. Something, well, 'fashionable' is too trite a word but for a first name, something 'of the times' reflecting the tastes of the era into which we were born. A name that will probably mark us out for ever as coming from a particular generation, whether we like it or not. A second name usually follows – perhaps after someone significant, a grandparent, or a kindly friend, and maybe a name with a nod in the direction of tradition or religious affiliation, a Mary or a Joel, say. And after all that there are nicknames, bestowed on us by family and friends with a casualness that takes no account of the opinions of the hapless recipients. Stig, Toots, Kiddo – not the kind of names you put on your CV. Finally, of course, if you're female you can fall for a fabulous guy with a totally ridiculous surname, and then what do you do? Well, most women still opt to change their names – solidarity triumphs – but they haven't exactly a range of choices.

So it's the small adjustments we can make to our names that become our own markers of new phases in our lives. The 'cool' versions of the name our parents gave us – like Jools or Zac, the add-ons we've worked for and prize – Doctor or MP, the adoption of a different spelling or a foreign equivalent of our birth name – Caite for Kate, Andre for Andrew, and, for that matter, Paul for Saul. These are slight but significant choices and we make them not only to project a different image of ourselves to others but in some way to alter our own concept of our identity, of who we are and what we might become.

For some people the change is part of a process, marking a stage in growing up or in pursuing a chosen way of life. For other people, quite a minor-sounding name change can actually signify a positively seismic shift in the way they are.

I love it when people I know well begin to call me Ruthie, not Ruth – it hardly sounds any different, but to me it's another name entirely: gentle and relaxed. Saul's new name Paul may well have been adopted for convenience as he went forth into the Roman world, but he used it always in his letters and I suspect he felt more comfortable - more truly the self he had become - as Paul.

*

They did it, in spite of everything! In spite of huge uncertainties and parental anxiety. Youthfully trusting in the essential goodness of life, Charlie and Melissa got back together. Not that they announced it with a fanfare of trumpets or anything, but they were just obviously, unstoppably a couple. It was clear for all to see in the way they looked at one another, finished one another's sentences, casually held hands, exchanged banter, made plans. And this time around, it was grown-up stuff. Serious issues were discussed, heads together at the kitchen table. So many questions, so few answers, but a determination to be together, now and in the future. No more teenage tantrums or Olympian sulks over nothing in particular, but earnest exchanges about how to get to a position where they could share their lives. Solemn discussion of subjects that, given Charlie's condition, could still only be aims and aspirations. Subjects like work and careers, saving proper money, getting a home, having children. They wanted it all – and why not?

We, their parents, couldn't help but be won over by the sheer intoxicating power of our children's love and optimism. They taught us a valuable lesson in the endlessly renewable energy of life, honestly lived, and our sceptical, middle-aged hearts would lift whenever they were around.

*

For there are times when all the carefully constructed argument in the world just crumbles in the face of plain, unvarnished honesty. That's how it was for the clever, disputatious man, Bar-Jesus. But I'm jumping the gun. First I have to get Barnabus, Paul and John Mark to Cyprus as planned – initially to Salamis and then across the island to Paphos, the seat of the Roman Governor, Sergius Paulus. That there were thriving communities of Jews on the island is evident both from Acts and from secular records, and amongst the Jewish element, there were already some adherents of the Jesus movement.

It seems *(Acts 13: 6-12)* that the Governor had become interested in aspects of radical Judaism, as he invited Barnabus and Paul, together with a Jewish mystic called Bar-Jesus (that is, son of Joshua) to explain their ideas to him. *Acts* dismisses Bar-Jesus as a sorcerer and a charlatan, but as Luke admits that Sergius Paulus was thoughtful and intelligent, it seems pretty certain this 'sorcerer' was an articulate, quick-witted man who, in the three-way conversation described, was deriding and cleverly ridiculing the teachings of Barnabus and Paul.

Whatever it was that actually sparked Paul's angry, authoritative response, it appears that Paul ceased bandying words and in the most forceful of terms, condemned the man's self-seeking twisting of the arguments. Whereupon Bar-Jesus, thus cursed by Paul, was apparently struck blind. Well, literally blind or not, the point of the story is surely the power of honesty, truthfully and assertively expressed, to cut through the most devious, most sophisticated word-play; that honesty is itself a transparent force that needs no supplementary argument to carry the day. Sergius Paulus, we're told, was seriously impressed.

It was clearly a source of considerable strength. Though Paul could, and sometimes did, argue the hind leg off a donkey (witness his letters) he could also, with confident ease, state his convictions with utter directness and total honesty.

I think nowadays, with our increasing dependence on visual images and 'spin', we're in real danger of losing our grip on straightforward, down-to-earth talk. The skill of spinning, of using exactly the right words to put a good gloss on bad news, to make empty claims or hold out false hopes, to grab undeserved praise or to minimise mistakes, is today considered an essential ability in politics and business. How long before it invades all our interpersonal relationships? Is it already creeping into our everyday lives? I can hold up a guilty-ish hand. I justify my spinning, of course. I'm not into serious deception, and to look at things in a different light often helps to oil the wheels of problem-solving, doesn't it? But there's the rub. I'm sure spin becomes a habit.

We shift our perspective relentlessly until it sits easily with our pre-conceived ideas, and then argument becomes futile. But when serious decisions need to be taken or intense disagreements have to be resolved, the habit of spin undermines us. We, with our high regard for clever debate and persuasive manoeuvring, so easily under-rate the extraordinary power of 'unspun' upfront honesty.

I fall into this error, I know. Yet I also know that when I'm brave enough to speak as calmly and honestly as I can, my words have an impact that far outweigh any feeble attempt I might make to twist them to fit a hidden agenda. And that's it really, isn't it? Honesty requires courage, for it can open us to ridicule or blame, and how often are we up for that?

*

The Inquest into the death of Charlie's flying instructor was necessary but awful; a long, harrowing day. Charlie gave evidence to an attentive, considerate Coroner's Court and in the breaks talked quietly with the young man's subdued, bereaved parents. Melissa was with him throughout, Peter and I were too, plus our sensitive, level-headed local solicitor who spoke to the court briefly but was there, mainly for Charlie's support. We all ended the day wrung-out and desperately sad and Charlie slept fitfully with exhaustion in the car home.

The hearing occasioned a certain amount of local publicity and a day or two later, Charlie was interviewed on TV. Of course, little of a fairly substantial interview made it to air, but Charlie's feisty attitude towards his own wheelchair-bound present and still-uncertain future came across loud and clear, as did his lack of bitterness and gratefulness to be alive. We were told he was 'inspirational'... and there were approaches from other journalists who wanted to feature his experiences in their own media. What to do?

It was up to Charlie, of course. He discussed it with friends and family and procrastinated, weighing up the pros and cons. If it were true and he really *was* inspirational, his story could maybe do some good. On the other hand, both we and he knew he was still a long way from physical health and habitual optimism, and the last thing he needed to become was a fraudulent hero.

In the end the situation resolved itself through the caution he exercised. A week or so of delay and he was old news. The journalists fell away and Charlie quietly decided that at some point of his *own* choosing, he would try to make good use of his newsworthily dramatic story and his ability to talk openly about it. At some point he would try to repay some of the enormous debt he owed to the doctors, nurses and physios who were now working with increasing confidence to reconstruct his shattered body.

That was that, then. A brief puff of publicity with its reassuring message of other people's interest and concern, and then ... the prospect of a long, hot summer, with Charlie confined to a wheel-chair, waiting for bone to grow and scars to heal. There were times, many times, when despondency and lassitude overwhelmed him and his nearly-found balance was temporarily lost. This diary entry, for instance:

Charlie fed up and tired after physio, Peter fed up and tired after long day in Cardiff. Over supper Peter railed at Charlie for his lack of direction and enthusiasm. Charlie snarled back that his current situation hardly inspired enthusiasm. Me, miserable between the two of them.

And a bit further on:

For the last two weeks, I guess, Charlie has been quite withdrawn, and recently he's been quite rude and unkind as well. I'd begun to feel that whatever I did, I couldn't get it right. I had to know if I could manage things better.

Going to hospital outpatients today gave us a chance to talk on 'neutral ground'. What Charlie had to say wasn't thought-out and wasn't particularly tactful, so it was difficult for me to get to the heart of the problem and face it. But this, I think, is what it's about. Charlie must be vastly more independent. Until he can take up the reins of his own life he cannot begin to sort himself out. He cannot begin to make plans for a future with Melissa. Well, yes, we understood that all along and were trying to encourage him to do just that. <u>Too hard.</u> The more we encouraged, the more we encroached on his life, his decision-making, his ability to act independently. To the extent that, now, we're starting to actually undermine his self-esteem.

So: we must stop this interference masquerading as 'encouragement'. We must accept that he'll have to take control of his life AT HIS OWN PACE. We must throttle right back and give him – and he and Melissa – a lot more mental privacy. Also, we mustn't forget to talk about ordinary things!

This week, I'm helping Charlie move from his little bedroom into the big guest room where he can spread himself out more. It starts from there. We must accept that Charlie has to move things along for <u>himself</u> and we must give him the space and the freedom to do it.

*

And I'm reading now of another big move out of the comfort zone into new territory where the Jesus movement was completely unknown and there were few friends to help. From Cyprus, Barnabus, Paul and John Mark set sail for what was then Galatia and is now modern Turkey, and travelled inland to the Anatolian town of Antioch in Pisidia. The region is considered somewhat off the beaten track nowadays but I gather that at the time of the Roman Empire the province, with its capital at Ephesus, was peaceful and prosperous and many small towns flourished along its overland trade routes.

This step out of the comfort zone seems to have cemented a crucial re-balancing of the partnership between Barnabus and Paul *(Acts 13)*. Hitherto, Barnabus with his experience and high-standing in the early church, seems to have led the expedition, with Paul and young John Mark in support. Now, when Luke writes of their mission, it's Paul who appears to be doing the talking and leading the way. Perhaps this had something to do with his determined courage and the absolute confidence with which he preached his faith. Or maybe it was the confrontation with Bar-Jesus in Cyprus that actually shifted the balance between the two men. Anyway, from here on, the relationship was subtly different.

Not that I suspect Paul actually took charge, (although my fat book of commentary on *Acts* would have it so), rather that the partnership was now very much an equal one.

I think this because later in the journey, at Lystra *(Acts 14)*, a crowd gathering in the wake of a healing, decided Barnabus and Paul must be none other than Zeus and Hermes in human form. Barnabus they thought was Zeus, the chief of the gods, and therefore Paul, they reasoned, was Hermes, his messenger and spokesman.

This, I reckon, was a perceptive view of the way the partnership probably now worked. Paul was busy, enthusiastic and organised, while Barnabus, older and certainly calmer, must have possessed a gravitas, a real presence in order for the crowd to have hailed him as Zeus. They operated well together, a complementary relationship that proved able to take the Jesus movement into the wider world.

Here I am, back to thinking about leadership again. There are different kinds of leadership, and as an organisation grows and develops, it demands different kinds of people at its head to move it forward. And it takes a leader with both sharp intelligence and generosity of spirit to know when it is time for him or her to begin handing over some of the power and the decision-making to leaders-in-waiting with different abilities. It's a known fact that when interviewing candidates for a job, interviewers will always prefer the people who are most like themselves – irrespective of the job spec or the needs of the organisation. And this is where dreams of expansion can founder.

I know someone who had experience of working with a small company funded by a university to get a brilliant, high-tech invention into the market-place. One of the main problems was, though, that the boffins whose 'baby' this was, wouldn't let go. They didn't themselves possess the commercial drive or the speaking ability to go out, make business contacts and publicise the amazing ingenuity of the product, but they couldn't quite trust anyone else to do the job for them. Result? It went right to the wire – to the point where the company almost folded – until economic realities prevailed and the erstwhile leaders of the project were persuaded to return to their university desks and entrust their 'baby's' development to new leaders with market-place skills.

Barnabus, however, was not precious about his status or his leadership – which is, quite frankly, amazing to me. I'd have grimly hung on in there and trounced the young upstart! But Barnabus seems to have realised that Paul had gifts he himself lacked and abilities the mission needed. That he never cow-towed to the younger man is evident from the argument that eventually ended their partnership, but not before a huge amount of valuable ground-work was achieved by these two men, co-working productively with the consent, be it tacit or explicit, of Barnabus, the intelligent, generous former Chief Exec. That's how I see it anyway. Barnabus, in my view, was an astonishingly honest man.

*

Progress! Clinic appointment today. Charlie can start to use one crutch in his left hand and put his weight through his right leg – which will be possible again when the current infection is under control. At last, both X-rays are good. Bone in right arm has more-or-less healed, but needs care. Leg now has continuous bone, if very slender in places. The frame has to remain for a consolidation period of 4 – 6 months. Charlie thinks that's ages, but it isn't, though it does mean it'll be winter before the frame's removed.

In other ways, I think the fog is beginning to clear. Charlie is decision-making. In the autumn he's going to apply for 'milk-round' positions in London – career jobs for new graduates anyway – for entry next summer. That's a whole year away and he should be fit by then! If he's ready for work beforehand, he'll take part-time and for cash. He and Melissa want to rent or buy a flat in London, preferably Battersea where they know people, and they're going to start looking at possibilities pretty soon. We've just completed a Benefit application which, hopefully, should give Charlie a basic income for the next 6 months so that he won't have to rush prematurely into a job.

How comforting it is to have a plan! A good, workable, adaptable plan. And the encouraging thing is that it emanates from Charlie – Charlie and Melissa, I should say. All the time things have been sensitive and difficult at home for Charlie, Melissa has been there for him. Not pushing, not 'cheering him up', just being. And now they're looking ahead. They're brilliant. They'd been talking about spending a few days in France in September, and Pete and I were thinking we could give them a lift and perhaps have a break ourselves. Now, however, they've decided they want to get on with things rather than just sit in the sun. And actually, I'm not sorry. Though personally, I confess to a profound desire for a holiday, this mood of 'can do' is a hugely exciting step forward. And the weather is glorious here anyway.

I'm going to dig out my big Italian pasta bowl in a minute and fix us a lemon and tarragon chicken salad to eat outside, with crusty bread and a bottle of white wine from the fridge.

*

Charlie was becoming impatient to re-join the world, to do all the things his able-bodied friends were doing – but he was, inescapably, different from them. His old identity no longer fitted, and, whether he liked it or not, he found himself having to chart his own course forward.

*

I'm struck by something similar in *Acts.* Christians were different, and these differences were gradually bound to have consequences. Yet, the early Christians were Jews and there was no intention amongst the leadership to break away.

'Men of Israel and you who worship our God, listen to me!' Thus, Paul addressed the Sabbath day gathering in the synagogue at Antioch-in-Pisidia (*Acts 13*). Paul was a Jew in the Pharisaic tradition. His speech clearly assumed from his listeners a solid grasp of the Hebrew scriptures. His training as a Pharisee would have been evident from his manner in the synagogue and his approach to theology, and in Antioch-in-Pisidia (as in all the other towns on his first journey) he initially received a respectful hearing. Pharisees were admired.

I've read quite a bit about Pharisees and most of it doesn't square at all with the bad press they receive in the gospels. On the whole they were scholarly men. They applied an intellectual rigour to their interpretations of the law and the prophets, but combined this with a care to seek the *meaning* of scripture in order to apply it with kindness and common sense. Of course there must have been plenty of individual Pharisees who became puffed up with pride and swaggered around, full of self-impor-tance. Jesus would have detested such hypocrisy. But within the Jewish tradition, Pharisees were held in high regard. Paul himself was proud of his Pharisaic roots and there is a school of thought suggesting that Jesus, too, might have been a Pharisee. Interesting, that. There do seem to be parallels. And Jesus certainly taught 'the Golden Rule': *'Do unto others as you would have them do unto you: that is the Law and the Prophets...'* just as Rabbi Gameliel's grand-father Hillel had famously emphasised before.

So Paul was given a hearing, and it seems that quite a number of his listeners were intrigued and wanted to know more. He was asked to speak again the following Sabbath, but before this could happen, conservative members of the congregation, who were clearly appalled by what Paul and Barnabus claimed, whipped up a protest to put a stop to any more discussion on the issue. A near-riot ensued and Paul, Barnabus and John Mark were thrown out of the synagogue, out of the town.

It became a pattern, wherever they went. At first the Jewish community seemed impressed with the Christians and gave them leave to speak. Quite quickly, however, the main body of the synagogue would weigh up this new message and conclude that however persuasively it was preached, the message itself was at best flawed and at worst, downright abhorrent.

As a Christian, I have to take this on board. Two thousand years of propaganda portraying the Jews as rigid-thinking, hard-hearted enemies of Christianity have succeeded in glossing over the very real difficulties involved for anyone thinking afresh, to embrace the Christian faith. So what was the problem? The problem was – and is – Jesus. Not what he taught, but who his followers thought he *was*, and what that might mean.

As far as I, a non-theologian, can tell, Paul didn't go as far as to claim that Jesus was God. I think that depends on how many of the epistles one credits to the authorship of St Paul, but perhaps I'm wrong on this. He did, however, proclaim that Jesus was the Messiah, the Lord's anointed, and not a king or a soldier but a wise teacher and a suffering servant. No serious difficulty here – I guess this would actually have been the intriguing bit, along with the shocking part of the story which related how this charismatic figure had been opposed, arrested and executed in the most brutal fashion known to Roman law.

There would no doubt have been more resistance to the climax of the story, where God himself was said to have raised this messianic figure from the dead, though Paul in his letters always preached a spiritual resurrection, not any kind of resuscitation, so that his disciples were able to experience his presence after his death. Indeed, Paul himself had experienced it.

Then the most interesting part of all: Paul taught that through prayer and through the simple shared rituals of eucharist and baptism, Christian Jews had found themselves able to identify with Jesus and feel for themselves his continuing presence in their lives.

This notion would, I guess, have been unpalatable to many mainstream Jewish believers, smacking, as it must have done, of a worship of the dead not a million miles away from the distasteful but flourishing official divining cults of former Roman Emperors.

And from queasiness to rage would doubtless have been a small step once Paul had moved on to his final theme: that through the Christian's identification with Christ, and not through the Law, men and women could find salvation; could find God... I'm not all that surprised they threw him out, to be honest.

Furthermore, as Christian doctrine in the years that followed became ever more prescriptive, so Jewish abhorrence became increasingly automatic, until the two religions, which, though different, have, in truth, so much in common, became implacably opposed. That's tragic, isn't it?

*

Peter and I are having a break after all! Tim arrives tomorrow – he's taken some holiday to be with Charlie while we're away. I hope they have a jolly good time without us. They both deserve it. Sarah will be 'on call' too. She's magnificent – but then, she has the built-in advantage of being a woman!

Physically, Charlie's pretty well at the moment. He's just been put on permanent antibiotic cover and it's transforming his life. Without the recurrent infections he can get on with putting weight through his leg and mobilising with one crutch. He's now walking short distances out of doors – not far, admittedly, but alone! A milestone.

I am, of course, a little bit uneasy too. The last time I went away I came home to …oh, I can't think …   But suppose I didn't let him out of my sight, what use would that be?

   Pathetic. No, I'm going to relax and I firmly refuse to feed my anxiety. If possible.

*

As Paul, Barnabus and John Mark were thrown out of Antioch-in-Pisidia, having achieved just a few Christian converts, Luke has them making the bold, unequivocal statement: 'We now turn to the Gentiles.' Which of course, they did – and they didn't. The pattern remained. Wherever they went, they made contact with the synagogue first.

I peruse quite a chunk of narrative (*Acts 14*).

At the town of Iconium and then at Lystra the experiences of Antioch-in-Pisidia were repeated. Indeed, at Lystra, there was such hostility to Paul that he was stoned. His body was dragged out of town and left for dead. But his new Christians, we're told, formed a ring around him there, and he revived. The next day he and his companions left for Derbe, and as elsewhere, a small Christian group, a church, independent of the synagogue and different from it, was left behind.

The return journey of the apostles to their original base of Antioch in Syria took them through Pamphylia, where John Mark left them. Some traditions say he left to accompany Peter on a journey to Rome. Others think that being young and under-standably overwhelmed by his experiences, John Mark simply bottled out and went home for a bit of normality. Paul and Barnabus continued on to Perga, Attalia and thence by sea back to Antioch. The mission of the Jesus movement to share its religious insight with all who would listen – be they Jew or Gentile – was well and truly under way.

And I'm thinking it seems incredible that these tiny churches founded so rapidly, and in the teeth of opposition, should have survived at all. But they did. Paul must have been an extraor-dinary man to have inspired such loyalty and commitment. I too easily think of him as irascible and pugnacious through the grumpier parts of his letters, but face-to-face he must have been full of warmth and encouragement and capable of gentle under-standing too. And though I know he had to top-up his teaching incessantly, he must nevertheless have possessed an astonishing ability to tune into the religious doubts and questions of both the Jews and the pagans of his day.

*

I'm worrying again about the appropriate fate of the scruffy diary: the diary of Charlie's miracle. This exercise in slow-reading *Acts* in conjunction with those entries, has allowed me to get further through it than I've ever done before ... well, without skipping bits. But when and if I finish, should I stash the diary away again or should I bin it?

I've thought about throwing it away so many times, but it's a hard thing to do. It contains dates, facts and thoughts. Surprising how quickly you forget the order of things. And the sheer number of operations, with all their attendant clinic and physio appointments, is quite staggering. I shouldn't want to forget that entirely. And then, the thoughts ... raw and painful with whole paragraphs of melodramatic self-pity. Yet, on the other hand, I'm heartened, considering the circumstances, by how many entries are really quite sane and even wise. There are bits I can read with objective approval ... and other bits I can scarcely read at all.

I guess that comes close to the point. The diary was never written to be read; it was written to be written. It began as an ordinary note-book in which I recorded only dates and facts. Then, as the weeks went by, I began to add comments and then thoughts, until, by the summer, when the weather turned oppressively hot and Charlie was stuck in his wheelchair, battling infections, I used it as an outlet. A couple of times a week I would pour out my thoughts and emotions and feel better for having done so. It was useful then, but is it still useful now?

I return to the fact it was never meant to be read. It has no literary merit whatsoever and is so intensely personal that my interpretation of events must surely verge on distortion. For instance, it reads as though Charlie, nothing and no-one else, was my only concern for month upon month. Oh, I mention in passing Peter and Sarah and Tim and the things that were happening in their lives, but the diary makes it seem like these were side-shows to the on-going drama of Charlie. That's not how it was, and I'd hate for them to read it and get the idea that that's the way I felt.

The diary does describe one weekend when Charlie was visiting Melissa's family. Sarah and Tim came down to stay. We went to a restaurant for dinner – Mum, Dad, and our two eldest, and we laughed and talked ... and talked ... and talked. Back home we sat up late into the night recollecting the events of the last few months and retelling aspects of the story from our own points of view. It was magic and I said so, but I guess even here the narrative's subject was Charlie, albeit offstage.

Which leads me to another issue. In my diary, I'm cast not merely as Charlie's chief carer but as virtually his *only* carer – and that's rubbish. Peter was a practical problem-solver and a father so proud of his courageous young son that you'd really have thought at times he was going to burst.

Sarah stayed in big-sisterly phone contact with her brother the whole time. She was a brilliant listener, defusing tensions and dispelling grumpiness when Charlie was at his lowest ebb, and her talk was bubbly: full of wit, warmth and fun.

Tim was somehow always there when you needed him. He never fussed or flapped, never got snappy or irritable. His off-the-wall humour kept us going and, like Sarah, his big city lifestyle gave Charlie a window on the world he was fighting to re-join.

And if I'd been allocating proper diary space to crucial people, then Melissa would have been on every page. Her life, her career, her hopes and expectations were turned inside out by my son, who, at the time of his accident, wasn't even her boyfriend. As she and Charlie grew ever closer, the rest of us began to appreciate what a truly remarkable young woman she was. She made the difficult, the unpleasant, the unlikely, seem perfectly do-able, and Charlie rose to her challenge to make things happen, for both of them.

But, my diary was *by* me, *for* me and *about* me, in relation to Charlie. It wasn't an account of clever people or key events, just my own preoccupations as I struggled to keep my tired, confused head above water. I suppose if I'd been worried about others reading the diary I'd either have given family and friends a more prominent part in it, or excluded them completely. As it is, they wander in and out like bit-players in a second-rate movie, and I couldn't bear it if anyone were to think this is how it was, or how it seemed to me.

So probably, at the end of the day, the diary will be cast away, its purpose served. Perhaps at Easter, if I've finished this project, I'll think again. Perhaps this is really what I'm doing it for.

* * *

GIFTS

A miracle is a gift; the greatest gift one could possibly be given. Since I'm not a fan of the supernatural, I'd say it was a gift of nature. Perhaps in these instances nature is disturbed by infinitesimal changes in the normal course of events, each tiny occurrence in the chain, building to produce a wholly surprising outcome. There may be ways in which the 'divine spark' in an individual can react with his or her circumstances and spur a miracle on, but I cannot believe in a directly intervening god. Why would such a god intervene for my son and not for the sons of others? It wouldn't bear thinking about. But still, a miracle is a gift. And once you've received a gift it's yours to do with as you wish. To use or waste it, to learn from it or forget, to develop it or not – and if to develop, then for good or for ill.

The thing is, I feel, although a miracle itself is an amazing and wonderful happening, it may still produce unfortunate results down the line. For handling a miracle is no easy task. We none of us receive any preparation or training for it. We may joyously embrace the miracle, but make a complete hash of our lives in its aftermath. Quite likely, really.

What we need above all is help. More gifts, in fact. The gifts of other people's time, their care for us, their judgement. If we are lucky enough to have friends or family – or professionals – who will give us this help, and if we are humbly (or reasonably humbly) able to accept it, we may possibly survive the miracle and emerge better people. We may even emerge in good enough shape to give usefully of ourselves to others. Exalted hopes.

I know only too well that when your life has been turned upside down, it's not so easy to see how you're ever going to be half-way normal again.

*

It was good for Charlie to be with his brother. They lazed around and talked and drank beer (even though Charlie was on antibiotics) and kept the house ticking over.

I don't suppose they thought of us at all, but, from the peaceful greenness of the Dordogne, I thought of them constantly.

*

Nothing and no one grows unaided. The Jesus movement was no exception. Its expansion depended upon the enthusiasm of committed individuals to spread its ideas. But the leadership in Jerusalem eventually found itself having to make horribly difficult decisions about what gifts of commitment were necessary to make someone acceptable as a Christian.

My slow-reading arrives at The Council of Jerusalem (*Acts 15*). Its Burning Question was that given the increasing number of Gentiles who were seeking to formally commit themselves to the Christian way of life, what should they to do in order to 'belong' as fully as their Jewish-born counterparts?

There was disagreement amongst the brethren. Although Judaism had never been a proselytising religion, it had always attracted converts, for whom the way in was clear. Becoming a Jew involved submission to the Torah (including all its detailed dietary rules) and acceptance for males of the surgical rite of circumcision. So it stood to reason that this remained the only true path to full membership of the community of Christian Jews, didn't it? Many of the early Christian leaders thought so. After all, Jesus himself was a Jew who worshipped in the Temple and obeyed the precepts of the Law.

But the movement had not stood still. The 'Way of Christ' was now being taken up by people whose knowledge of mainstream Judaism was at best sketchy. Were they going to insist that new Christians should fully convert to a religion – even when Jesus had gone out of his way to criticise its outward symbols of conformity? Some voices were raised in fierce disagreement against the 'traditionalists' – notably Paul's; and there were some apostles who wavered – notably James.

The next step? A conference: known to history as The Council of Jerusalem, and I like this bit, so I expect I'll be boring about it. I remember studying it all those years ago at school and thinking it was incredibly tortuous and tiresome. But later, as a history student, I returned to it whenever 'decisive' councils came into view.

Convened by the church in Jerusalem, it reads in *Acts* as a highly-charged, passionately argued debate, whose clear-cut outcome altered the course of Christianity. But reading between the lines later on in *Acts* (and looking at Paul's own recollections in his letter to the *Galations*) it was only in retrospect that it acquired the mantle of such a pivotal meeting. At the time it must have been a passionately quarrelsome and painfully divisive gathering, whose conclusions remained in doubt for many years.

Being a British Christian I can't help being reminded of the Synod of Whitby (664 AD): that great confrontation between the Roman Catholic and the Celtic Christian traditions in these islands. Recounted by the Venerable Bede, he puts all the relevant arguments in the mouths of the protagonists at the debate, and in the end, the high point of the drama comes when the final, irrevocable judgement is handed down. In the case of Whitby, that decision went the way of the Roman Catholic tradition. In the case of Jerusalem, it was the radical stance of the missionaries to the Gentiles that carried the day.

In real life, however, it seems that neither conference was quite as coherent or decisive as either Bede or Luke would have it. In fact in both instances, the rehearsal of all the major arguments, the involvement of all the important players in person, and the articulation of a firm, considered judgement that was to hold for all time, was almost certainly a narrative device. Of course there was a meeting, or meetings. For sure the main characters attended more than one, and yes, the arguments were forcefully presented on both sides. And decisions were eventually hammered out.

But in neither case were they decisions that took immediate or universal effect. For though in the early church, decisions could be promulgated, compliance could not be assumed. Enforcement wasn't even a possibility. Cooperation was the best that could be hoped for and that could only be obtained by continuing persuasion. This was the case in 7th century Britain too. And after Whitby, in Ireland and much of the west of Britain, Celtic practices persisted for generations – centuries.

As for the Council of Jerusalem, well, Paul, who was actually present, at least for some of it, clearly did not feel himself bound by its pronouncements in their entirety. Nevertheless, the very fact that these councils took place at all, testifies to a challenging period, which resulted in the changing of Christian mind-sets. It testifies to a vigorous and forward-looking church, unafraid to confront the realities of the world in which it found itself and seeking opportunities to present its message as a living, developing gift in the most practical and effective way possible. Perhaps I'm over-egging the pudding a bit, but it rather puts our tentative, defensive apologies for a spiritual life today to shame.

Back to *Acts*. There seem to have been three distinct lines of argument presented to the elders of the Jerusalem church. The first came from a group of former Pharisees who had become Christians. They were horrified at the disrespect shown to the Law by believers who were in the habit of sitting at table with their uncircumcised Gentile brethren and eating 'unclean' meat with them.

Before I write this view off as illogical and prejudiced, I must take into account the deep hurt caused by slighting anyone's religious rituals or practices – be they superficial or profound. I'm aware, for instance, of the way my Roman Catholic friend squirms when, accompanying her, I enter a church and fail to cross myself with water from the stoup and genuflect to the altar. She knows that most Protestants don't make these gestures and that I would feel self-conscious and false if I suddenly adopted them. She certainly doesn't consider me less of a Christian for my different approach, but – and it's a big but – I sense her mild shock and I know that in a small but important way, I'm disregarding the ancient tradition of her church. Outward signs of respect are precious in all our dealings with one another.

Having listened to the pharisaic contingent's views with compassion, however, it seems that the elders of the Jerusalem church were convinced by the refutation of their position which Luke put in the mouth of Peter.

Peter's view appears to have reflected the standpoint of the majority. He vouchsafed from his own experience that Gentile converts were encountering the Holy Spirit in exactly the same way as the disciples themselves had done. They were, therefore of equal standing in the church and, beyond their initial teaching and baptism, they needed to undergo no further rite of entry into the Christian life.

Paul's reasoning (given his earlier-written account of the dispute in *Galatians*) went further. He believed that the merits or demerits of the Law were beside the point. The point being that enlightenment, salvation, knowing God – put it how you will – was to be found in identifying oneself wholly with Jesus Christ. That, and nothing else.

This last line of thought appears in *Acts* to have been accepted by the Council. Only, subsequent events clearly indicate that it wasn't really. There remained a strong 'Judaising' faction within the early church, enlisting sympathetic behaviour from the likes of Peter and also of Barnabus. Paul's powerful, radical stand on the subject of the Law may possibly have moved minds but clearly did not change hearts. That took much, much longer.

For the Council, in weighing up the arguments, it seems the apostle James played a key role. For he was the one prominent person who is said to have changed his mind. Initially a conservative, he nevertheless listened to the 'progressives' and was swayed. His courageous change of outlook apparently swung the mood of the Council and they finally decided that Gentile converts need not become fully-fledged Jews.

In practice, however, the issue continued to be debated. As far as Paul was concerned, the Law had become irretrievably bogged down in the pettiness of men, but there was a clearer, simpler path to God. Paul believed that finding Jesus, the Christ, was the way to find God. The Law, in this regard, had been superseded. To some people, this was an extraordinary and liberating idea, to others, it was just plain scandalous.

So the vexed question of whose gifts were acceptable, of who could be considered a 'real' Christian, rumbled on. But irrespective of the arguments, new people kept coming and their gifts were gratefully put to use.

*

I've suddenly realised that there's almost nothing in the scruffy diary about the development of Charlie's thoughts on continuing his pilot training. And, if it doesn't sound far-fetched, I'm maybe reminded of this by slow-moving councils, because in making his own important choice, Charlie groped his way towards a decision which crystallised gradually. And there was a gift.

Amongst his many visitors when he was in hospital were instructors and student pilots from his flying school. And from his hospital bed, Charlie was determined to fly again as soon as possible. Once discharged, he was taken up, twice, I think, as a disabled student. I certainly remember him coming home full of beans, confessing he'd been scared but describing how he'd taken the controls and flown – straight and level – around the local area. Then, he'd actually been able to relax as the calm, kindly senior instructor had carried out some basic manoeuvres. All in all, the flying school had been understanding, and his return to the air was positive.

Flying as a potential career, however, was another matter. In the first place, he'd had the time to begin pilot training because a job he'd been offered after university had failed to materialise. Working in a restaurant and later at the airport to keep financially afloat, he had had unexpected time to start lessons and just enough money to fund them.

With his father's RAF background, aircraft had been part of the scenery of Charlie's childhood, so the idea of his getting a private pilot's licence seemed a pretty natural goal for him to aspire to. A few lessons in, and Charlie was enjoying himself, and he was actually thinking about entry standards for airlines. And then the plane crashed.

Somewhere near the start of the long, hot summer-of-the-wheelchair, Charlie was visited by a friend of a friend. Like Charlie, this young man had had a serious accident during flying training. It had taken him a long time to regain fitness, to resume training, get his first licence and finally to land a job. Major airlines had turned him down and he was working for a small freight company but he was accumulating valuable experience and was utterly confident about a career in aviation. He made a big impression on Charlie.

After this meeting, though I couldn't say exactly when it was, Charlie came to some conclusions.

He'd enjoyed his flying and when he was lying in pieces in hospital he'd been extremely keen to get back up in the air again. However, having achieved that, he was less sure about his desire to continue. A degree of fear was probably a factor, as his body became more 'together', but fear was temporary and could have been overcome. A more compelling reason to abandon his pilot's licence, was his determination to build a life with Melissa, and to make a serious career move as soon as possible.

Finally, I think that it was listening to his young visitor that clinched it. This tenacious young man's accident had occurred several years previously but he was still not back on track with his career as a pilot. And Charlie simply did not possess the same burning ambition to fly. He'd loved the sensation of the freedom of the skies. He had found mastering the basic techniques of flying extremely satisfying, but he was not obsessed with it, neither did he really know the extent of (or lack of) his natural ability.

Given his situation, he would need at least as much determination as his visitor if he were to get back into flying. Being honest with himself, he admitted he didn't have that single-mindedness. He had not cherished boyhood dreams of becoming a pilot. He'd simply begun lessons for opportunistic reasons and it had been an adventure ... but there the adventure would have to end, he decided, and real life would develop differently.

*

OK, but the hard facts of the case now were that Charlie was a disabled, unemployed arts graduate, who wasn't at all sure what he wanted to do. Not a brilliant starting point, but there were clues. He was a 'people person', articulate, organised, energetic. PR, marketing and sales were obvious possibilities, but he wasn't sure – he was still a bit sore from the PR company who'd offered him a job and then let him down.

He trawled through piles of careers information, and with increasing exasperation he declared whole areas of employment non-viable. Maternal comment was given short shrift. If jobs were interesting they required many more years of study. If they seemed to offer financial independence, chances were they were 'boring'. Family meal times were frayed affairs, for what seemed a long while. Until ...

Years before, Charlie had expressed a passing interest in working in the City. This was kind-of outside our collective family experience. We knew no one in banking or broking, or even accounting for that matter, and somehow the seed of this particular idea had never germinated. Now, he found in his bookcase a slender paperback he'd acquired at the age of about thirteen, entitled *How the City of London Works*. He devoured it in about half an hour. Intrigued, he set about acquiring more detailed, grown-up information and soon he was beginning to turn various possibilities over in his mind.

*

And then, in contrast to the positive tone of my scruffy diary, I read in *Acts* that there was an almighty quarrel. Life is never going to be smooth! For all its restraint of language, the narrative of *Acts 15:36-41* indicates quite a spat.

Once again, it turned on the uncomfortable matter of whose commitment was acceptable and whose not.

Paul and Barnabus, we understand, returned to Antioch to deliver the decision of the Council of Jerusalem on the standing of Gentile converts in relation to the Torah. It seems that Paul was also anxious to revisit their little groups of Christians in Galatia. Barnabus was clearly of the same mind, but the two men fell out over the question of whether to invite John Mark to accompany them again. For reasons of his own, John Mark had pulled out before the end of their previous mission and Paul was therefore insistent he should not go with them again. Barnabus, who seems to have been more open-minded and forgiving, and more willing to take a chance on someone (after all, he was the one who was prepared to take a chance on Paul himself) judged differently.

He was not going to be bulldozed by Paul and stoutly maintained that if John Mark was not to be one of the party, then he would not go either. There was no room for compromise and so the two men made different plans. Paul chose a man called Silas to be his companion, while Barnabus decided to take John Mark to work with him in Cyprus.

I think, though, there was almost certainly another dimension to the quarrel – deeper and less easy to argue. I think it hinged on the continuing difference of approach between Paul and Barnabus to the vexed question of respect for the Torah. Paul's letter to the *Galations* suggests that Barnabus was unwilling to condemn the traditionalists who found it impossible as Jews to share the sacred ritual of eating at table with 'unconverted' Gentiles. Sounds just like Barnabus to me – generous and non-judgemental.

But actually, I'd say Paul was right and he was wrong. This was a fundamental principle, worth fighting for. Paul's letters indicate that on-going divisions within the Christian brotherhood between Jewish and Gentile converts did institute a kind of apartheid that caused ugly friction and bitterness between and within the new churches. Paul was adamant he'd have none of it. He was right – but it cost him his friendship with Barnabus. The John Mark thing, I suspect, was simply an issue over which they could respectably agree to differ.

It's a shame that when the time came for Paul to leave his old colleague, he doesn't seem to have been able to do so amicably and with heartfelt good wishes for Barnabus' mission. We know that Cyprus became an increasingly strong base for Christian communities and that over the centuries it has retained a steadfast Greek Orthodox tradition, despite wars, conquests and internal divisions. The island boasts enough dedications to St Barnabus to assume his work bore much fruit. I'm glad. Certainly Luke gave this generous man a good press, perhaps derived from his own research, perhaps from Paul's later memories of him. I like to hope that even though Paul, hot-tempered, single-minded and uncompromising, seems to have parted company with Barnabus with stubborn words and without a backward glance, in later years his appraisal of the man might have been happier, more rational and sincerely appreciative of the huge contribution he made to the early church.

*

Paul and Barnabus, both setting out on new journeys. Charlie, as the scruffy diary recounts, was doing likewise, he meant what he said about career stuff. Oxford University's careers centre allowed this graduate from a different place to stumble around their premises, his frame and crutch taking up more than a fair share of space, consulting their up-to-date information and making phone calls. Once he was on the career trail, word of mouth brought him useful information from individuals too. On more than one occasion friends gave him tip-offs about firms who were looking to recruit, and letters of enquiry duly went into the post. He was lucky to be able to tap into such a willing support network.

But it's a demoralising process, looking for work. You get your hopes up, only to have them dashed. You want the job – but they don't want you. Or the position sounds great in the advert but when they send you the whole story the snags become all too obvious. Charlie's search was no different. Most firms he wrote to were simply not interested. Although he crafted his letters with great care, presenting his fight to regain health and fitness in a wholly positive light, there was no getting around the fact he was currently disabled. But he kept going, often disappointed but undeterred. This was real, solid progress. He was clearly psychologically ready for work – if only his physical condition would catch up.

Charlie's many letters of application and enquiry yielded only two positive responses. But, what the hell, you only need one job – and one of the responses was from a ship-broking firm in the City. He was very, very excited. The letter invited him for an interview, and he accepted without a moment's hesitation, despite the fact that the date they specified was really too soon for him. For he was once again battling against pin-site infection. His leg was horribly sore and the early date for the interview was not going to give him time for things to improve much. Nevertheless, he wouldn't ask for another date. He would, he stated resolutely, manage the interview somehow.

And he did manage. He gratefully accepted his father's help, and together they planned the mission with military precision. So, early in the morning on the day of the interview, long before it was light, Charlie began his bathing, frame-cleaning, washing, shaving and dressing routine. Walking was excruciating but, leaning heavily on his crutch, he could manage half a dozen paces or so at a time.

Peter was up similarly early, scraping a mild October frost from the car windscreen, while I, in my dressing gown, brewed coffee and made toast. It was still dark when Peter loaded the wheelchair into the car and they set off for London.

I gather they made it to the City in reasonable time and found a place to park somewhere near the Baltic Exchange. It was light when Charlie got into the wheelchair (how he hated it by then, but he couldn't have walked) and Peter pushed him along the crowded early-morning pavements, weaving their way through the city workers, to arrive outside the offices slightly ahead of schedule. So far, so good. There was no way Charlie was going to attend his interview in a wheelchair, so, leaving his father, he gritted his teeth, went inside and bestowed his bravest smile on the young woman at the Reception desk...

He was there for a couple of hours, being interviewed by several people in succession and shown around the offices. Questioning was sharp, he told us later, although everyone was charming. No one made much of his leg, though his walking became more and more painful and more obviously laboured as time went by. Peter said that when he met Charlie again outside the building, he collapsed into the wheelchair in a pale, exhausted, dishevelled heap. But he was clearly pleased. The day had gone as well as it could have done.

*

Paul needed help too, setting out for the Anatolian mainland with only Silas in support. To his credit, he knew he needed help, and this, his second major journey, seems to me to be particularly marked now by his willing acceptance of the gifts of others: their time, their talents, their friendship and their material contributions to the cause.

First among these was Timothy, from Lystra. Well-thought of by the brethren there and in Iconium, Paul was obviously impressed with him too. *Acts (16:1-5)* doesn't relate how much persuasion Timothy required, but the next thing we know, he was agreeing to accompany Paul and Silas onward, from town to town across the Anatolian plain.

And that's not all Timothy agreed to. We're informed that, before he left, he underwent the rite of circumcision. Given all the fuss that had surrounded the deliberations of the Council of Jerusalem, and given Paul's dogged insistence that circumcision was absolutely not necessary, this action seems quite astonishing. But was it?

You see, I think this is where I can so easily get Paul wrong. Paul, who was so energetic, so quick-tempered and outspoken and was clearly a swift reactor to circumstances – did not do theology 'on his feet'. As a thinker, his letters reveal a very different kind of man: deliberate, logical, profound and extremely subtle. He seems to have possessed a rare mixture of traits that makes it impossible to pigeon-hole him as this or that type of person.

And as far as his Judaism is concerned, I think it's been all too easy to misunderstand his position. For Paul was a Jew. And though he didn't see any necessity for Gentiles joining the Christian brotherhood to first convert to the mainstream practice of Judaism, neither did he advocate that Jewish Christians should renounce their Judaism. Of course Christians interpreted their religious heritage in a distinctive and decidedly non-traditional fashion, but there was no question at all that any of them – Paul included – should imply that the Law or the Prophets had become worthless. And it seems to me that it was Paul's continuing devotion to Judaism – albeit in a radical form – and his extensive knowledge, use and sincere love of the Hebrew scriptures, that succeeded in anchoring and defining Christianity for testing times in the future.

Timothy was well-placed to be a bridge between the older, Jewish Christians and the newer converts from paganism. As his mother was of Jewish birth and his father was a Gentile, so both Jews and 'Greeks' could identify with him. His particular gifts of understanding would make him an invaluable advisor to Paul and an asset to the mission. To be a bridge, however, he would need to be taken seriously by the Jewish elders in the synagogues – and so, willingly and pragmatically, Timothy decided on circumcision.

I like the idea of Timothy as a bridge, especially as my own son Tim has grown from a fiercely determined child, convinced of the unique importance of whatever project or craze he currently favoured, into a balanced, thoughtful adult – quite a 'bridge' sort of person himself. Anyway, Paul's Timothy appears again and again in the various epistles that follow *Acts* in the New Testament. Bringing him on board was clearly a shrewd move.

*

The smile on Charlie's face as he waved his letter in the air said it all. He'd been offered a position! The ship-broking firm really wanted him! He was beside himself with relief and happiness. On the phone to Melissa, he talked for ages, a little about the past, he said, and a lot about the present and the future. When he emerged it was with an even bigger smile. They'd decided to chase the small Battersea basement she had found for possible conversion. It would take quite a bit of time and a great deal of effort, but it could be that they'd found a home for themselves.

There was never the faintest chance that Charlie would turn his job offer down – but there *was* a snag. They wanted him to start the following month. They understood he'd have to go into hospital at some point to have the Ilizeroff frame removed, but they wanted him to join them before Christmas. Well, there was no point in Peter or I protesting, but Charlie was clearly not in a fit state for a 9.30am – 7.30pm day. His recent bout of infection was back under control but he was still in significant pain and it sapped his stamina. Nevertheless, we comforted ourselves with the thought that he'd only be working for four weeks or so until the Christmas break, and around that time he was due to have the operation. He was young, we reminded one another, he was absolutely determined and somehow, he'd do it.

Melissa, meanwhile, had worked like fury and secured the Battersea basement. Permissions were granted for its conversion into a one-bedroom flat, contracts were exchanged, and she set about planning its transformation from a dark, dank storage space into a proper dwelling with sitting room, bedroom, kitchen and bathroom, all tiny, and a pocket-handkerchief of a walled garden. If things went well, they could have a home of their own by the spring.

*

It's difficult, in my opinion, to maintain an emotionally intimate relationship with someone you love, if they move to a location too distant for unplanned visits. The prospect of Charlie's centre of gravity shifting to London was hugely exciting but it also signalled to me the inevitable diminishment of the unusual degree of openness that had, for a while, existed between us. Absolutely right and healthy – but those few months of real closeness, despite their ups and downs, had been precious to me, and I knew I was going to miss it dreadfully.

*

Paul's new journey began by retracing his steps. He'd left his little churches in Galatia after a relatively short time and was warmly welcomed on his return visits. But he wasn't planning to stay; he wanted simply to see his old friends and then be off again to pastures new.

It seems to me, as I read *Acts* alongside the scruffy diary, that 'full steam ahead' is where I find both Charlie and St Paul right now, and I can't help a small sigh because I know that ahead there lie wonders but also sorrows – and much hard work.

*

It took a massive effort but Charlie just about managed it. He moved to temporarily share his brother's flat in London and, commuting back and forth in ruinously expensive taxis, he started learning to be a ship-broker. Tim kept his anxious parents posted since Charlie wasn't even going to contemplate defeat. Apparently, every evening he arrived home exhausted and sore – and goodness knows how much pain-killer he consumed – but he was utterly determined and, with help from his brother and his girlfriend, he kept his head above water.

Just before Christmas, the Ilizeroff frame was finally removed. This was psychologically huge, since the frame had both protected and facilitated the mending of Charlie's leg and he'd become accustomed to its support. But it had also caused no end of pain – and embarrassment too, as he was routinely stared at and had constantly to combat the feeling of being a freak.

The op was a success and the bandages were removed ... to reveal, oh no! ... a pathetic stick-leg. The frame had given it a kind of artificial symmetry and solidity, whereas in reality, the leg was wasted and thin and slightly bowed. Furthermore, it had gorey great holes in it where the pins had been. Melissa almost fainted and Charlie was shocked and unhappy. He could also hardly walk, even with a crutch.

Physios were brilliant, though. Very enthusiastic. He was given another load of exercises and lots of reassurance that his muscles would rebuild really rapidly. He came home from hospital in a reasonably optimistic frame of mind and was determined to enjoy his few weeks off work.

Christmas was absolutely magic! Charlie's leg already improving and everyone together – laughter, singing, games – wonderful! For New Year, Charlie and Melissa went to Suffolk with friends. Charlie drank too much and walked too far, and Melissa was not amused ... but they seem to have made their peace again! They now have the keys to the flat in Battersea – with everything still to do to it!

*

Charlie had found his balance. He'd still have a long way to go and many difficulties to contend with, but the way ahead was clear now and he was moving with an assurance and a maturity that belied his years. I was so proud of him, so pleased to see him with Melissa – and pretty satisfied with my own contribution to their hopeful situation. But just as Charlie got himself firmly back on to the beam, I contrived to fall right off it.

Just as everyone else seemed to be forging ahead with cheerful confidence, I lost the plot. Or perhaps it was *because* everyone else was full of renewed vigour. From being hugely needed, practically and emotionally, I found myself very suddenly on the sidelines. Charlie and his support team of family and friends had won through. No longer did his accident dominate our lives; the hurly-burly of everyday existence gradually began to preoccupy the others, as it should, but not me.

I was enormously pleased for everyone. Sincerely so. This was what I'd been wanting with all my heart and working towards for the last year. Now, here was Charlie, mentally balanced, emotionally whole and physically improving fast. And I knew that my love and care, and my professional social work expertise too, had enabled me to be an architect in his recovery.

Now, however, I felt redundant, and emotionally, I felt vulnerable and useless. I couldn't help but think I had completed the most important task I would ever face, however long I lived. Never again would I have such a responsibility, and never again be so confident that I could *do* this thing that was demanded of me.

Today, Feb 5th, I took Charlie's wheelchair and his perching stool back to the hospital. Our hall looks vast without the chair sitting there. A time of new beginnings.

I tried to pick up the threads of my own life. I tried to work, tried to think positively, but this Lent, a year on from the miracle, was cold and bleak. I could bask in the reflected happiness of my family, but, as for myself, I could see no particular purpose in my continued existence. I realised this was irrational and ungrateful – wicked, even – but I could do little about it. I functioned at a lowish level, prone to tears and reluctant to plan ahead, but I simply could not seem to inject a sense of purpose back into my life.

And while part of me reasoned that this was probably a perfectly natural reaction to the extraordinary events of the previous year, its draining persistence did worry me. I sporadically attempted to fight it, not asking for help but putting on a brave face. It didn't work. Worse still, in not talking frankly to anyone, I denied myself the gift of the compassionate attention I so desired and so desperately needed from others. Meanwhile, those I loved, loved me in return; they were considerate and gave me space. But I couldn't seem to heal myself.

*

Luke was a healer (*Acts 16:10*).

At Troas, the port of embarkation from Asia Minor to Europe, an individual joined Paul's party who was clearly the source for this part of the story. Suddenly, the narrative switches from the third person 'they' to the first person 'we'. The tradition is very ancient that this individual was Luke. Luke the doctor-friend of Paul, mentioned in the epistle to the *Colossians*. And if so, this could make him the same Luke as the author of the *Gospel* and *Acts*. Perhaps. Of course, scholars will continue to debate the point and we're unlikely ever to know for sure. But while I don't think it matters greatly, it's an appealing thought that gives me a sense of immediacy in Paul's travels from here on.

Paul's Luke was a physician, he was a God-fearing Gentile. Luke, the New Testament author, was similarly a Gentile. He was Jewish by faith but a Gentile, writing in Greek for a Gentile audience familiar with the Septuagint. This Luke cast his net widely as he researched his work, and certainly he incorporated large chunks of pre-existing writing, from the *Gospel of Mark*, for instance, which he proceeded to make his own.

He was a superb storyteller. Of course his book is a product of its time and place but it's amazing! Crammed full of pen-pictures of astonishing people, with events tumbling one after the other, from the sublime to the bizarre. And *Acts* is unique. I mean, we have gospels other than Luke's, but apart from *Acts* there is no other surviving account of Christian beginnings. Maybe no other was ever written.

In any case, Paul seems to have been well pleased with the new man who joined them at Troas, whoever he was. Are we greedy, wanting to flesh out the shadowy genius known to us as Luke? To imagine he could be both the hardy, seafaring companion of Paul and the sensitive, painstaking author of the great literary history of Jesus Christ and the early Christian church? I guess it's just human, wanting to project a solid identity on to a well-loved author. Do you read with intense curiosity a dust-jacket biography of the author of a book that absorbs you? I certainly do. And I study the photo. I know it tells me almost nothing ... and yet, it is a link.

So, Luke relates that when Paul and his friends reached Troas, they were at a kind of crossroads. There were land and sea routes to any number of places. Where to head for? Apparently, as Paul was weighing up the options, he had a dream in which he saw a Macedonian beckoning and asking for help, and so, Macedonia it was ... And, immediately the text runs: 'We set sail for Macedonia'. Was it Luke – Paul's Luke? – the author Luke? – who gave of his time and his energy to become one of the little band of adventurers? Tradition claims that it was.

*

I couldn't heal myself and in the end, I became a burden – most particularly to Peter – and it wasn't fair. He'd worked so hard, he'd kept going, he'd solved problems and supported us all without question. And in focusing intently on Charlie I had neglected him – no two ways about it – but he had understood. In the months following Charlie and Melissa's move into their flat he'd accepted that I needed time to get my act together, and he was fed up, but patient. Eventually, however, my listlessness and reluctance to do as he had done and throw myself into work, drove him to distraction.

Our family, which had been so close, now seemed intent on becoming a collection of individuals moving swiftly onwards and outwards. All three of our children were negotiating new jobs and moving into new flats. Their young lives under way again.

Peter was involved in international conferences and was quite often away. And I should have been getting myself back on track like everybody else, but I just wasn't.

To me, work seemed pointless, I seemed pointless and, by extension I suppose, it seemed to Peter that I considered our future pointless as well. This couldn't have been further from the real truth, but at the time I felt pretty dire and, feeling nagged, I could be stubborn and silent. No wonder he worked ever longer hours, drank a glass too much wine of an evening, fell asleep in front of the television and barked and snapped at me. For my part, consumed with self-pity, I sometimes cried, but mostly, I retreated into a world of impractical daydreams that I was busily constructing as a barrier against the harsh necessity of making a new start. For quite a long time, we drifted on like this, finding it harder and harder to communicate truthfully, sensing deepening difficulties between us, but too weary to tackle them.

And then, one Sunday, clearing away the breakfast things, Peter said he couldn't go on like this.

"Like what?" I think I asked, not realising at first how very serious he was.

In order to tell me, he needed to get angry, and having psyched himself up for the job, he let fly with harsh words and stinging accusations.

Dismay and resentment surged through my brain. For though there was no doubt in my mind that I loved Peter and would always love him, I was not under any circumstances going to stand and be shouted at. I turned on my heels and left the room:

"So this," I thought, with gloomy resignation, "is the end, is it?"

"A long and fruitful marriage. Over?" And it was largely my fault. But obstinacy kicked in. I wasn't going to beg or plead … I simply felt unbearably sad – and empty.

Why didn't I talk to someone – anyone - for heavens' sake? Why didn't I rant and rave and weep and demand sympathy? Because … because I'd been a beneficiary of the most extraordinary and precious event that can happen to anyone: a miracle. And though I hadn't coped well with our family's return to 'ordinary life' there was no way I'd have wanted anything else.

So, I told myself, there was nothing to be done and no point in seeking out 'shoulders to cry on'. Proud, ridiculous, a singularly unintelligent sort of vanity. There are times when all of us need help. But there I was, middle-aged and miserable, and quite unable to ask for it..

*

It was a woman who gave Paul the help he needed to get things up and running and establish the first Christian community in Europe. This was in Phillippi in Macedonia, where Paul and his companions knew nobody. At a place by the river, just outside the city gates, a group of Gentile women were in the habit of meeting on the Jewish Sabbath for prayer. Amongst them was a woman named Lydia.

Today, reading *Acts 16* I'm astonished to find that the narrative directly concerning Lydia actually only occupies two verses – the final sentences of the chapter. She clearly played a crucial role in the mission to Macedonia and she's an important and colourful character in Luke's story, so I'm rather surprised to find, not two chapters or so, as I was expecting, but a mere two verses. It makes no difference, though. The portrait Luke paints of Lydia is vivid and his few words speak volumes.

I remember Lydia from my Sunday school days. She made a big impression on me. My ten-year-old imagination conjured up a tall, exotic, beautiful woman, clothed in shades of purple and wearing exquisite golden jewellery. Having been told she was a merchant of purple dye, running a business and a household of her own, I realised even at that tender age, that she would have been a woman to be reckoned with. Therefore, in my imagination she was a rich, intelligent young widow who had bravely overcome the death of her (rich, intelligent) husband, to single-handedly provide a secure and comfortable life for her small (beautiful, intelligent etc.) children and her band of devoted servants.

Well, I don't retract any of it. In my mind, that's how Lydia was. She was a strong woman of good judgement, at home in the world of commerce, but generous and kind, and full of intellectual curiosity.

There were other God-fearing women at the place of prayer in Phillippi but it was Lydia who quickly understood and responded to the challenge of the ideas embodied in the work and life of Jesus of Nazareth. She, with her household, was soon baptised – the first 'Greek' Christian we know of, who actually came from ancient Greece. And her home, into which she welcomed Paul and the others, became the first Christian meeting place on mainland Europe.

Quite a woman, Lydia. For me, she remains one of the most appealing characters in the story of Paul's journeyings, and I think Luke must have liked and respected her too, for those two verses tell us so much.

*

Quarrels are toxic. It's sad to think that Paul and Barnabus may never have patched up their quarrel. Perhaps, having gone their separate ways, they lost personal contact, and with it, all chance of mutual forgiveness.

My scruffy diary here becomes strangely distant and self-justifying, for Peter and I too, were wearily unforgiving. I returned half-heartedly to teaching English and was about as much fun as a wet Wednesday. Peter, meanwhile, gave up on communication and was more immersed than ever in his work. It was as though we'd both run completely out of steam and were simply holding our breath. I had never felt so uncertain.

And then suddenly, Sarah was there for me, unasked for, undeserved. Returning from Scotland to live in London, she immediately noticed and was dismayed at the threadbare state of her parents' marriage. It wasn't a matter of siding with me. The unsatisfactory relationship between Peter and I wasn't Peter's fault, and not for a moment did she or I try to pretend it was. But she was there, on the phone, or meeting for lunch or seeing me after work in London; listening to me, intently asking questions and patiently boosting my shattered morale.

Together we talked about the testing time Peter and I had lived through and our very different ways of coping with it. Essentially, Peter copes by doing and I cope by thinking. Working together, as we did in the early days after Charlie's accident, we were one hell of a good team. But during the long months of Charlie's recovery we had individually burrowed deeper and deeper into our respective ways of being and had actually ceased supporting one another, though both of us still desperately needed support.

Now, was it all too late? We didn't quite know, but Sarah intuitively understood that even though she could see I needed to take a leaf out of her father's book and start some 'coping by doing', any change would have to come from within me. So she didn't nag or warn or preach, she just kept asking what *I* wanted and refused to let me shift the focus of discussion away from that. Then, I would feel angry – not angry *about* anything, but angry, I think, at life, at my own ineffectuality. I didn't want to desire things because I didn't want to strive. Anger wasn't a pleasant emotion but it was at least a change from feeling empty.

Sarah didn't hound me – she unerringly sensed when to back off. But although she was only twenty-something herself, she kept a wise and compassionate eye on me.

She could wave no magic wand, could promise no happy ending but she could and did make me realise that I *had* to think about myself, that not to care was selfish: that care for others begins with a care for oneself. Her persistence may have been harrowing at times, but it was welcome nonetheless, for I knew it was essential. And bit by bit she began to undermine my miserable conviction that I was washed-up and irrelevant. Her attention started to make me feel valued again – not for what I could do, because plainly I wasn't doing anything of consequence – but only and entirely for the love I could still give. I hadn't rated my capacity for love, but she helped me to see it was the most important thing of all.

We lived uneasily for a while, Peter and I, tiptoeing respectfully around each other, smiling ruefully, not saying a lot. But I think Sarah spoke with him too, as we both seemed more able to view our situation from the others' perspective. And gradually, things got better.

*

During a short holiday in Cyprus – mountains and monasteries, lemon trees and Mediterranean warmth – I made a conscious decision to work to restart my life: to have a serious shot at coping by doing. And I determined that if I was still the person Peter wanted to stay married to, I would invest practical love and energy into taking our relationship forward. Peter's response was understandably cautious but I was able to be relaxed about that. And he seemed relaxed too. He was funny and kind and supportive in all sorts of ways, and I was appreciative. We were friends. By the time we came home a corner had been turned. There was still a lot to do; we still had to figure our future out, but somehow, we both believed we could, we would, make it together.

*

It's been hard, revisiting that period of my life when, in the wake of the immeasurable blessing of Charlie's recovery, I managed to fall apart. Bringing worry to my children and chronic disharmony to an erstwhile cheerfully supportive marriage, I had pulled the dark clouds down upon myself. But it wasn't self-indulgent, or even particularly self-pitying. For a short time I hadn't wanted to be myself at all. I'd seemed to want instead to be a spectator of life with no substance and no wishes of my own. In my memory it remains a strange and puzzling time and I was lucky to have my daughter's wise, gentle help to pull me out of it.

Fortunately, it did pass, before I destroyed the very relationship with Peter, that was, in truth, my anchor. The whole experience gave me a glimpse of the havoc that depression can wreak in people's lives. And I'm grateful for that, though I wish the learning hadn't been quite so painful.

* * *

GROWTH

Growth – real, sustainable growth, is surely not so much about size as about substance. If something merely grows larger it will eventually exhaust its strength and perish. To grow productively, anything – an organisation, a person, an idea even – needs to deepen and to connect.

I'm getting towards the end of the scruffy diary, I'm a long way through *Acts* and Lent is fast drawing to a close. But growth is firmly on the agenda. I'm astonished to have been able to read and digest the contents of the diary this far. And to my surprise, the factor that has most helped me has been the 'companionship' of the early Christians as they struggled to make sense of *their* miracle and shape *their* lives accordingly. There have been both striking parallels and quite obviously divergent issues to think about along the way, but I don't suppose I'd be this close to achieving my own small goal if I hadn't had their efforts alongside me, sometimes as a comfort, sometimes as a helpful distraction.

*

Easter approaches. Easter is mystical. Easter beckons, drawing me into a place, a state of mind perhaps, that is far from the everyday, and yet does not feel unnatural. Alongside all the springtime fertility stuff of eggs and rabbits, and the gleeful anticipation of a public holiday, Easter is an awesome festival. Its narrative is gripping and direct, in the way that powerful stories are instantly and universally recognisable.

From the entry of Jesus into Jerusalem, the menace of Passion Week accumulates, until it reaches its climax in the unremitting horror of Jesus' brutal execution by crucifixion. Classic tragedy ... but then the mind-blowing twist. They have not entirely succeeded in killing Jesus off. In some way, he is still there. And if you ask me, you can think about this conundrum until your brain aches but it doesn't do a bit of good. Miracles, as I well know, are not capable of intellectual resolution. 'Who Moved the Stone?' and 'The God Delusion' are equally irrelevant in my view, for Easter is driven not by scholarly thought but by mystery and awe. Personally, I suspect that these senses are profoundly necessary to human beings and quite remarkably dependable – and yet, as a child of my time, I still can't bring myself to trust intuition and instinct alongside the power of the mind for research and thought.

Furthermore, the church's teaching on Resurrection remains a problem for me – partly because I hate the *word*, with its overtones of 'restoration' and I'd really rather use a fuzzier, less definable term – and partly because I think that before a profound mystery, there can be no orthodoxy. As individual Christians we sense what we sense and our experience cannot be dictated or second-guessed by anyone – not by the Pope nor the Archbishop nor by our fellow-travellers on life's journey.

Before the enormity of Easter, I can identify with the ancient Buddhist practice of marking a sacred site with the 'footprints' of the Buddha. 'He is here yet not here,' they seem to say, and the mystery is not explained but experienced.

*

Celebrations: Charlie and Melissa went public, they got engaged. The first by a long way in their circle of friends, they were subjected to much anxious questioning, but they harboured no doubts and felt no obligation to apologise for their youth or their boldness. Their extraordinary ordeal had made them different, and being all too aware of the unpredictability of life, they were determined not to waste a moment of it. They planned a short engagement and a winter wedding in London. Wonderful!

It's strange, isn't it, the power of a decision to marry? Even today, when there's virtually no pressure on couples to take this step (and having taken it, small difficulty in undoing it again by divorce). The notion of a solemn commitment for life still invests the wedding ceremony with high drama, glorious romance and unforgettable hope. It's wildly optimistic but I know that every time I'm a wedding guest I willingly subscribe to the conviction that this will be a truly life-changing occasion, even though for most couples, it won't make a scrap of difference to their everyday lives. They'll already have slept together, lived together and experienced many of life's ups and downs together, well before they decided this was for keeps. Marriage has lost its *everyday* significance. It no longer marks having legitimate sex, living together and learning to share, as it still did when Peter and I were wed. But, divested of its practical advantages marriage has become simply, movingly and clearly about two people's faith in the enduring power of their love. Marriage nowadays is a huge leap that a man and a woman take together into an unknown future. And the very fact they don't *have* to do it, makes a modern wedding, in my book, incredibly moving.

*

Leaping into the unknown takes boldness and confidence, and cheek – chutzpah is the word I'm looking for!

After Charlie and Melissa's engagement, I go on to read about Paul's reaching out to connect with a new type of interested listener – the cultured, influential, educated pagans of the late classical world. A tall order. It must have taken deep thought to shape his message – and chutzpah to deliver it.

The place in *Acts* where Luke focuses on Paul as a communicator to educated pagans is in his speech at the Areopagus in Athens. He'd arrived in the city by way of Thessalonika, where he had established a small church with the help of the Philippian brethren. Arriving after that in Athens he found himself in a city, small now in power, but still formidable in its reputation as an intellectual centre, noted for its breadth and freedom of thought. OK, I have to admit straight away that Paul didn't exactly go down a storm with the Athenians but neither was he a complete flop. He acquired at least two noteworthy followers, and it is in Athens that Luke reveals something of Paul's approach to educated Greeks. Absorbing stuff.

So, as I read it *(Acts 17: 16-34)* here stands Paul, having gathered a crowd in the open air, pitching his ideas 'cold', to a totally unprepared audience. He begins by acknowledging the serious intellectual interest of his listeners in matters philosophical and religious, not flattering them but establishing common ground between them. Some, he knows, are followers of the Epicurean way and others are Stoics, and many of these describe themselves as seekers after the Truth to be found in an as-yet-Unknown God.

What he, Paul, wishes to declare to them is that this 'Unknown God' is not unknowable. That the one basis of all things – God – can be approached. As the source of all that exists, one way God can be approached is through knowledge of the wonders of creation, for God is not outside it, like the idea of gods whose idols represent divinities who inhabit another plane entirely, but part of it... *'in Him we live and move, in Him we exist.'*

This would certainly have resonated with his Stoic listeners, whose concept of the Ultimate was Mind; Reason that permeated everything, so that all life was sacred. It might also have intrigued some Epicureans who, as materialists, did not admit gods into the equation at all – but if by any chance the divine existed, it was unknown and unknowable.

It's fascinating, I think, how these two ancient philosophies remain so strongly with us today ... Epicurean materialism driving us to understand in ever-greater depth how our world, our bodies and our brains actually function, and Stoic spirituality continuing the elusive, compulsive quest for an understanding of the mystery of life itself.

I realise that, long before Paul, Greek and Judaic ideas had collided and begun to influence one another. It has been claimed in some quarters that Jesus himself was a Galilean peripatetic, peasant Cynic or that he was a teacher in the Stoic tradition. Over the top I guess. But the time seems to have been ripe for a meeting of Semitic and Greek insights, a synthesis for which Christianity became a powerful vehicle. Not that this prevented Christianity from absorbing many of the more superstitious and idolatrous tendencies of folk the world over – it did. But I would say that it also combined in enduring form, the loftiness of ideals and the profundity of thinking to be found in both Judaic and Hellenistic traditions.

The teachings of Jesus on the theme of The Kingdom and the theme of The Neighbour embody deep wisdom, accessible to both Greek and Jew in late classical times ... and, in our time, accessible to all. Or at least, that's how I see it. I suppose I've taken the thoughts expressed in *Acts* and put them into my own words – just as Luke must have taken the preaching of Paul and put it into *his* own words, for the benefit of his readers. All writers do it, no matter how objective they set out to be.

Where was I? Athens. Thus far in his speech at the Aeropagus, Paul seems to have achieved a respectful hearing. However, it is his subsequent assertion of the Resurrection of Christ that proves to be the stumbling-block for his Athenian audience. They scoff. And who can blame them? The miracle of Resurrection was always difficult; it was hard to comprehend at the time and remains so today. Our Epicurean materialism scorns the inexplicable while our Stoic sense of wonder admits to the existence of more than we can know, more than we can explain. Resurrection, though, is not an ideal subject for beginners ... and I'm not surprised that the Athenians, most of them, scoffed.

Paul's address at the Aeropagus, however, suggests that Christian philosophy set out from quite early days to engage in subtle Greek-style argument and the presentation of complex abstract ideas. And indeed, it seems that one of the chief reasons for the relative rapidity with which Christianity spread in late classical times was its growing appeal to the 'thinking classes' of the pagan world. So much for the possibly overplayed idea that Christian congregations consisted almost entirely of poor and downtrodden folk, so many slaves and women. Not the whole story, I'd say.

*

A sparkling, frosty morning. London bustling but not frantic on this final Saturday in December and we have a marriage to celebrate! Looking back, the whole day shimmers in my memory, with Charlie and Melissa at the centre of the action, extravagantly beautiful and happy. I remember the music – especially Grieg's exuberant 'Wedding Day at Troldhaugen'. And I particularly remember one of the readings – well-known, modern words by Louis de Bernieres describing married love so eloquently it takes your breath away:

Love is a temporary madness, it erupts like volcanoes and then subsides. And when it subsides you have to make a decision. You have to work out whether your roots have so entwined together that it is inconceivable that you should ever part. Because this is what love is ...

Love itself is what is left over when being in love has burned away, and this is both an art and a fortunate accident. Your mother and I had it, we had roots that grew towards each other underground, and when all the pretty blossom had fallen from our branches we found that we were one tree and not two.

And after the serious bits, the party! To everyone's surprise, Charlie and Melissa opened the dancing not with the expected romantic number but with a loud, upbeat Latino jive to which they danced with a raw energy that stopped us all in our tracks. They gave us a dazzling, gutsy, complicated performance. Carefully choreographed and thoroughly practised, it goes without saying that Charlie's part in it was considerably less dramatic than his wife's. Nevertheless, between them they put on a terrific display, Melissa's long blonde hair flying while Charlie twirled her away and then tugged her back into his arms, jiving as if their life depended on it. It was a gesture of triumph, a statement of intent. We, the wedding guests were captivated and amazed. And when they were through, panting and laughing – there were cheers to raise the roof!

I remember leaving as the party was drawing to an end. Funny, that, one seldom remembers the end of an evening but this one was magical. Warmly wrapped in our coats and cloaks, we stepped out into a clear, sharp, star-spangled night. Footsore and deeply satisfyingly exhausted, we climbed into our London black cab and sighed as we sank into its seats. Speeding off into the night, I was too tired to think but I knew that the afterglow of this wonderful day would warm us for a long time to come.

*

Step change. The pace of the scruffy diary from here onwards slows. Whereas, in the beginning, every dramatic entry was hastily scribbled, now each section is becoming longer and more thoughtful. I was using the diary less, more selectively, as my life stopped being lived in headlines. I was less frequently moved by events, but moved, I think, more deeply.

It's odd because at this point there's a step change, too, in the chronology of *Acts*. The pace of the actual narrative doesn't slow down but the time span covered does, quite markedly.

For now, Paul leaves Athens for Corinth, and for the first time, he stays long enough not only to establish a church but to nurture its beginnings himself. He was there for eighteen months, while Luke gives us a glimpse of yet another side to Paul: Paul the 'grafter'.

Growth doesn't happen without constant effort, much of it centring on mundane tasks. Growth is satisfying and being the leader of a successful team – as Paul was – is rewarding. But it is also hard, hard work.

Did he meet them by chance, I wonder, or did Paul have an introduction to Priscilla and Acquilla? *(Acts 18:1-11)*. His close friendship and easy working relationship with this positive, energetic married couple seems to have made Paul's time in Corinth a particularly productive experience.

It's great, isn't it, when you meet people with whom you can forge an immediate bond? People who see the world in much the same way as you do, so that huge chunks of the 'getting to know you' process can be skipped and in no time you're treating one another like old friends.

Paul had much in common with Priscilla and Acquilla. Like him, they were Diaspora Jews, living away from the region of their home. They'd come from Rome, where there was already a community of Christians, and they shared the same trade-skill as Paul: they were in business as tent-makers. So Paul lodged with them, visited the local synagogue with them, took them with him when he moved his small church into the house of Titius Justus, and for many months, until Silas and Timothy came from Macedonia to help the project, he worked alongside them to earn his keep.

To be useful; practically, immediately useful – as Paul, Aquilla and Priscilla were to one another – is immensely satisfying. As social animals, mutual interdependence is the key to our survival and well-being. We need to be needed, we need to use our skills for the benefit of others and we need to be appreciated. Usefulness to the community is the basic characteristic of a fully functioning mature adult and it is usefulness that distinguishes the healthy adult from the very old, the sick or the seriously disabled.

Inevitably, all of us will experience periods of helplessness during our lives and we will depend on others to care for us then, as we will try to care for them. Achieving maturity or returning to health, we relish being able to use our abilities and our energies in ways that will be appreciated by others. If you ask me, this isn't altruism, though 'going the extra mile' for someone else often is, it's biology.

Paul had a trade. As a tent-maker he used his hands to manufacture a product that was wanted and needed. Appreciation of his work was shown by the fact that customers were happy to pay him for it. Basic stuff, but the demand for a true craftsman endures.

I gather that it was obligatory in those early rabbinic days for a Rabbi-figure to learn a trade so that he could support himself when necessary and not become a burden to those he taught. So, alongside his academic studies, the young Saul had evidently mastered the marketable craft of tent-making. What a wise and practical tradition!

*

Paul, of course, was far from perfect. He was clearly a compelling communicator and, it seems, a warm and caring pastor. But his letters to the Corinthians – and other churches – suggest he never stayed anywhere for quite long enough. And after he left, much confusion would develop about matters of faith, of practice and of morality. Paul's was a driven personality and he continually moved onward, necessarily leaving the follow-up work to others – and Corinth, despite his eighteen month sojourn, was no exception. However, without the problems, we may never have had the letters ... so who am I to pass judgement!

*

It really didn't seem fair. Just as my psyche was returning to normal, my body complained – and how! I'd had arthritis mildly for years and on the whole it had been little more than a nuisance. But suddenly it flared up alarmingly. I was aching and stiff and my left hip began to give me serious pain. I ignored it for as long as I could but finally took myself off to my GP. I suppose my relatively young age plus the fact I'd not recently had much trouble, was the reason why at first, low key remedies were administered. Paracetomol and physiotherapy were the order of the day. But I knew they weren't working and I was getting worse. There were times when a short walk to the local shops would find me limping homewards in agony. And scarily soon after that, I found I couldn't actually take a single step without pain. My GP was horrified as I staggered clumsily into her surgery leaning heavily on a walking stick, clearly made for someone considerably shorter than myself. She was lovely; caring and immediately practical. I left with a prescription for strong anti-inflammatories, an appointment for an X-ray and a note authorising me to collect some crutches at once.

Ah, the prospect of crutches – a lifeline! I drove straight away to the hospital address on my note, thinking I had plenty of time to collect them before the depot closed for the day at 12 noon. But I hadn't bargained for the car parks – all completely full. Finally, at 11.50 I abandoned the wretched car by a grass verge and set off with my stick. How I'd have loved someone to have taken my arm and let me lean on them. But no one was about as I made my slow and painful way to the hospital entrance alone. Inside was even worse. Reception was unaccountably empty, so there was nobody to phone ahead for me. My heart sank, the minutes were ticking away. The depot was clearly signed but the corridors seemed endless and my footing was unstable on the polished floors. My uneven gait and gritted teeth began to attract stares from passers-by, but I was beyond caring, my whole concentration focused on getting to the depot before it closed.

Finally I arrived, collapsing in a heap just as they were packing up. I gasped my desperate request, pessimistically certain I'd be turned away, but I must have looked as unhinged as I felt, for a kindly young man sat me down, assured me I wasn't too late and brought me a glass of water. It's all a bit of a blur really … until the moment I was given my crutches. They were magic! I could move easily and without pain. I'd never used crutches before but they were utterly wonderful.

As I retraced my route through the hospital, the miles of corridor turned out to be only yards, and outside, the sun was shining. My car was where I'd left it – unclamped and without fines – and I was suddenly quite sure I was going to be all right.

Of course, I went on to make the mistake of all users of crutches – physical, mental or emotional – which was to think that my problem was solved and I could rely on them indefinitely. Unfortunately that wasn't the case. In the consulting room of the orthopaedic surgeon, I gazed at the X-rays of my left hip. I guess I thought I'd have some options: 'We could try this, or that' – some clever medication perhaps, with the prospect of surgery one day if it didn't do the trick. But the X-ray said it all. The joint was shot and a full hip replacement was the only item on the menu. We talked. I could see from the X-rays I have shallow hip sockets. The left hip had worn out. The right one had a way to go before it, too, would cause trouble. Oh my, I wasn't prepared for this. "And what about the rest of me?" I wanted to know: "My aching knees, my stiff fingers, my toes, my shoulders, my back? I'm falling apart!"

My calm, professional surgeon gently did his best to reassure me that once the hip was sorted I'd almost certainly feel the benefit throughout my body. 'Almost certainly' didn't seem great to me right then, but with shock turning to resignation, I booked a place on his list – as many weeks into the future as my cowardly reliance on crutches would take me. No choice.

*

By the time Paul felt the need to move onward from Corinth he was no longer young but had grown in maturity and experience both as a man and as a teacher.

One characteristic he seems to have retained from his youth, however, was an ability to keep learning from his successes and failures and to adjust his thinking and his plans accordingly.

So many of us in middle age seem gradually to think within comfortable, self-imposed boundaries; we tend to rest on our laurels and start to believe we have very little left that we must learn. What nonsense! But for myself, I'm well aware that growth, including personal growth, doesn't come without effort. For me it will require sustained clarity of thought, a willingness to move out of my 'comfort zone' and an unshakable sense of purpose if I'm to grow through my middle years, into a wise old age. Will I make it?

Paul learned well from the success of his long stay in Corinth and at his next stopping point, in Ephesus, he again put down roots, this time for about three years. Returning from Macedonia, with detours to revisit his Galatian churches, he determinedly set about building up a thriving Christian community and a solid working base in Ephesus, the leading city of Asia Minor. It seems he had decided on a steadier pace of expansion and a more involved – more fatherly? – approach to the development of his churches. This last and longest project of his journey has the look of consolidation about it.

With the sure touch of a good leader, Paul brought many of his team with him, to deepen and connect. Priscilla and Acquilla appear to have accomplished much of the set-up work, whilst Timothy and Erastus seem to have moved back and forth between Paul and the Macedonian communities. Paul who, I'm ashamed to say, I've always thought of as a bit of a control freak, was obviously a shrewd and willing delegator and there was clearly enormous loyalty and trust between him and his co-workers. I suppose it's the authoritarian tone of his letters that can give the impression of a man with a substantial ego but I need to remember they were written in another time and another place. Maybe I'm the one with the ego problem. The church Paul founded in Ephesus prospered and became an inspiration and a haven for many of the early Christians. Indeed, there's a longstanding tradition that Jesus' mother Mary and his disciple John eventually lived out their days there.

But I'm coming to *Acts 19:21-41*: the incident everyone remembers about Paul's time in Ephesus – the eruption of an almighty riot, led by Demetrius the silversmith. Luke's point in including it may have been to underline the astonishing growth of the Christian community in the city, to the extent that even the powerful pagan cult of Artemis/Diana felt itself under attack. Doubtless a bit of an exaggeration, but the riot makes for dramatic reading. A mob of angry craftsmen and townsfolk, taking two of Paul's companions hostage and hustling them into the public theatre, chanting: "Great is Diana of the Ephesians" over and over again. Paul was all for hurrying to the scene and addressing the crowd and had to be restrained Meanwhile, the rioters vented their anger at the threat these Christians posed to continuing healthy sales of

Artemis merchandise – notably, one imagines, the range of expensive silver statuettes of the goddess. In the end, aggressive feelings began to blow themselves out and a few calm, well-chosen words from a senior town official (reminding the mob that the whole world held Ephesus in high esteem for its glorious temple to Diana and that the crackpot behaviour of a few harmless foreigners was not going to change anything – or words to that effect) sent the crowds slowly on their way, their point made, the disturbance over.

I love the story; it speaks straight to my experience. I'm a city-dweller and I enjoy the hustle and bustle of the market place. Retail has low profit-margins and the smallest upsets to people's normal purchasing patterns can finish an individual trader – bad weather, hold-ups in supply, lack of credit, bad debts – not to mention vociferous Christians railing against your business on its very doorstep. So I have a certain amount of sympathy for Demetrius and his friends, although I know they needn't have worried - it was some time yet before the Diana/Artemis cult faded away. I have to admit that I also like the story because I have a soft spot for goddesses.

I'm not an ardent feminist but the endless masculine pronouns in the bible sometimes get me down and the odd goddess is a bit of a reminder. I mean, it's loopy to imagine that God is male. (Though millions of people do.) And by the same token it's equally daft to think of God as a woman. The reality of God has to go beyond the attributes of gender. But the pagan goddess as a personification of divinity is a reminder and a corrective, I think, for those of us whose culture has for millennia conceived of the eternal source of all that is, as male.

The Abrahamic faiths from the beginning emphatically rejected the metaphor of the great Earth Goddess and, arguably, in so doing, they seriously crippled associations of awe and splendour, power and might with femaleness. In our own isles, the Celtic goddess known in Ireland as Dana (the counterpart of Gaea), once a symbol of the immense power of nature to generate life or to destroy, dwindled into the sorry concept of witches and hags and evil aristocrats like Morgan-le-Faye. I think it was a great loss, even though we're talking myth and metaphor and definitely not God-as-a-bloke versus God-as-a-girl.

To be serious, the riot scene at Ephesus, so dramatically narrated in *Acts* should make us all think about idolatry, and to what extent our received ideas of the divine, cause us to imagine our God in the image of ourselves – or in our case, the image of our fathers.

*

Forget the hospital interlude. I was a hopeless patient, quick to believe my surgery wasn't working and sadly lacking in the fighting spirit department. Despite this, thanks to the skill of the surgeon and the support of a long-suffering physiotherapist, I found myself the proud possessor of a brilliant bionic hip. Quite the best-functioning joint in my body. And as I began, to my surprise, to recover and to walk again without tottering, I took stock.

I needed to get back into work but I also realised that with the continuing nuisance of arthritis I'd need to pace myself, certainly in the immediate future and probably always. Self-employment had been a good experience but its uneven workload – feast or famine – was seriously incompatible with a chronic medical condition. I was determined that arthritis was not going make too much difference to my life but my creaking joints did deserve the best I could give them. I was going to have to take gentle exercise, little and often, eat and sleep well, plan ahead and say "no" to open-ended commitments I couldn't control . How many of us resolve to do just that, and then break our resolution almost at once? In the past I'd been guilty many times over. Job-wise I always seemed to end up see-sawing between working my socks off and collapsing like a stunned mullet. No longer. I needed good, useful employment, with boundaries.

Which is when I came across the Probation Service advertisement for programmes tutors. When I qualified as a Probation Officer, some twenty-something years previously, there were no such things as probation programmes. But in subsequent employment as a social worker (in those days the qualification gave entry to both disciplines) I'd always chosen to be involved in group work, and in my self-employed phase I'd taught students and run workshops. The notion now of having a job that consisted entirely of delivering cognitive-behavioural programmes to small groups of offenders was truly exciting. On the downside, even part-time hours would be mostly in the evenings and I knew from past experience there would always be pressure to work harder and longer than the contracted hours.

I thought about it, and decided to apply. I was sure I could do it competently, and if I got the job it would at the very least be a challenging start to a new phase in my working life.

In the event, they took a chance on me. With no recent experience of Probation, I attended the interview leaning heavily on a crutch, only too aware that I was hardly going to look promising. However, I was so completely convinced that right now, the job was for me, I must have talked the panel into giving me a shot at it.

I turned up at the office on the first day with some trepidation, telling myself that if it didn't work out, there were plenty of other things I could do. This was because between the interview and the start-date, former colleagues had been warning me darkly that the Probation Service was not what it was. Its ethos, they said, had changed beyond recognition from our 'Advise, Assist and Befriend' days to become first and foremost an arm of the penal system. And I was not certain I was going to enjoy that. Yet the minute I stepped through the doors, I felt comfortable. Within half a day it was paradoxically clear that although everything was different, nothing had changed. The structure of the service and the legislative framework within which it operated was completely new to me, but the people were just the same. Exactly the same mix of colleagues that I remembered, with exactly the same pressures, grumbles and worries; the same hopeless idealism tempered with periodic bouts of cynical gloom. As I paid my contribution to the office coffee fund (Fairtrade of course) I knew these people really *cared*. It was lovely to be back.

And the Probation programmes were rewarding. It's not a job for everyone, of course; unsocial hours, constant monitoring of performance, last minute alterations to schedules, but its twin demands of teaching and group-work were perfect for me. I liked my colleagues and I liked the offenders too. All of us are flawed individuals. Some people have committed illegal and even wicked acts, some people are violent and can be dangerous, but no one is evil through and through, and no one is incapable of change. And that's not sentimental rubbish, it's the truth.

*

Paul had said quite early in his stay at Ephesus that he wanted to return to Jerusalem for a visit in due course, adding: '*After I have been there, I must see Rome also*'. But it was some time before the planned trip took shape. The main purpose of the journey was to be the safe delivery by Paul in person of a collection for the church in Jerusalem. Paul had sought donations from all his churches and the collection had reached significant proportions. He was no doubt proud of his congregations' generous response and was keen to touch base again with what was still 'the mother church'.

When the time came, Paul's farewell to the churches of his great missionary journey was solemn, dignified and touchingly personal. I read with delight the story of Eutychus *(Acts 20:7-12)* for it describes a small miracle, quite modest on the 1–10 miracle scale: a 2 perhaps? Like Charlie's.

At Troas, the port from where he had embarked for Europe, a young man named Eutychus sat up late into the night in a crowded room, listening as Paul spoke and fighting sleep as he perched on a windowsill. Finally, overcome by sleep he fell out of the window and plunged three floors to the ground, where he appeared to be dead. Paul, we're told, *'seized him in his arms'* and assured the company there was still life in the boy – whereupon they returned in relief to the house, broke bread and continued to talk until dawn. Eutychus survived his accident. I wonder what he did with his life after that? I wish I knew.

Paul's final farewell took place at Miletus, close to Ephesus, where a large assembly of elders and members of the churches came to see him off on to his ship for the first leg of his journey to Palestine. Paul was certain that his destiny was calling him back to Jerusalem and he felt that, whatever happened after that, he would not see these friends and co-workers again. The leave-taking was intensely moving. Paul spoke with the company about his part in the work of spreading the gospel and their responsibility to now hold fast to the teachings. Then he knelt and prayed with them. And then, as the moment of departure approached: *'there were loud cries of sorrow from them all, as they folded Paul in their arms and kissed him,' (Acts 20:37).*

How can I continue to think of Paul as a proud, combative, and curmudgeonly man? Why do I so easily forget how warm a personality he was? How loving and friendly, how inspiring and exciting?

As the ship pulled away from the shore the comment: 'We parted from them' indicates that one of Paul's companions on the next stage of his journey was Luke.

*

As the fifth anniversary of Charlie's plane crash loomed, he announced a collection of his own. He wanted to mark the anniversary by doing something special to raise money for the orthopaedic hospital that had overseen his reconstructive surgery. For himself, he wanted to attempt something physically and mentally challenging, and for the hospital, he wanted to make a donation that could really help. And for his family and his friends he wanted to show how their love and care had borne fruit. For he was once again a whole, healthy and useful member of society.

I don't know for how long he had been incubating the idea but it seemed that in next to no time he'd set up a web site. On it was a 'flyer' to download, dominated by a colour photograph of the tangled wreckage of the Cessna plane that had appeared in the local paper. At the bottom left-hand corner, a small head-and-shoulders picture of Charlie emphasised the personal nature of his appeal:

On 4th February five years ago I was involved in this light aircraft accident at Turweston Aerodrome in Buckinghamshire. Crashing soon after take-off, the pilot and I were cut out of the wreckage by fire crew and I, the lucky one, survived and was flown to the John Radcliffe Hospital in Oxford. I was saved by the intensive care team and put back together by three very talented surgeons supported by hundreds of dedicated hospital staff. After 15 reconstructive operations involving my arms, legs and abdomen and 7 months in a wheelchair, I was back on my feet.

On 4th February this year I am aiming to run the 21 miles from Turweston Aerodrome in Buckinghamshire to Oxford Airport, the intended destination of the flight 5 years previously.

The reason for the flyer is of course to raise money for a charity, namely the NHS Nuffield Orthopaedic Limb Reconstruction Unit, who specialise in rebuilding limbs that are severely broken or deformed. I am greatly indebted to them for saving and rebuilding my right leg and if I complete the run it will be a testament to their skill and professionalism.

If you are able to sponsor me, let me know by return e-mail or call me on the number below.

Charlie Jolly

The venture was launched: Charlie's thank-you. Charlie's gift.

*

It occurs to me that from here, Charlie's own story gets lighter while Paul's darkens. But both are about growth. Charlie's personal growth was wrapped up in a joyful gift that sought to connect with all limb-reconstruction patients like himself. The growth that Paul's actions assisted was not personal – his life was endangered and his freedom was curtailed – but it gave energy to the growing and flourishing of the Christian movement itself.

I read how, on his way back to Jerusalem, Paul stayed with the evangelist, Philip. Last mentioned in Chapter 8 of *Acts* he was known as the founder of the church in Caesarea and Paul's visit is a reminder of how small the Jesus movement still was, and how relatively tightly-knit its organisation.

In spite of Paul's generous and valuable collection for the Jerusalem brethren, right from the start everybody seems to have had misgivings about how he would be received. Attempts to persuade Paul to think again, however, were in vain and he pressed on with the journey overland in order to arrive in Jerusalem in time to celebrate the feast of Pentecost.

In the beginning things went well, Paul was cordially welcomed by James and the elders of the Jerusalem church. But they, too, were worried about the safety of their controversial guest and (as *Acts 21:18-36* relates) with good reason.

The name of Paul had become associated with the simplistic notion that he and his followers repudiated Mosaic law and advised Gentile converts to ignore its precepts. This wasn't an accurate interpretation of Paul's position, but it was a 'shorthand' that stuck, because he was indeed in the forefront of the faction that released Gentile converts from the rite of circumcision and adherence to the Jewish dietary code.

And I guess all this goes to show that the rift between the Judaic brethren and the independent Christian communities of the Gentile world was growing wider – notwithstanding the deliberations of the Council of Jerusalem. It was still not clear whether 'unconverted' Gentile followers of Jesus would, in practice, be accepted by their Jewish counterparts as many Judaic Christians saw no reason to change their rigid stance on the issue. They were obviously afraid of what they thought Paul stood for, and during the springtime festivals of Passover and Pentecost, Jerusalem was full of Jewish pilgrims from all over the empire, fervently attesting their membership of the faith. No wonder James and the others were concerned for Paul's safety.

In these circumstances, it seems Paul was persuaded to take a Jewish vow that involved the shaving of his head – an action that would indicate to all who saw him, that, for himself, he remained an observant Jew. It didn't do the trick though. He was recognised, and, given his reputation as a 'Gentile-lover', it took no time at all for those out to get him to convince a mob that he had taken a Gentile into an inner court of the Temple.

Paul was seized, a disturbance ensued and the Roman guard was quickly mobilised to arrest him for his own protection.

It's sad, isn't it, how the formal structure of a religion comes so rapidly to overlay its essential purpose. Clearly, what you do and what you believe are two vitally important elements in any religion. Many of us who've been through atheistic and agnostic phases in our lives have sought to throw out all our traditional baggage of belief and practice and start with a clean sheet – only to discover that with no baggage at all, we're adrift without an identity or a starting point. But the issue of 'belonging to the club', evidenced by acceptance of its canon of beliefs and practices, becomes inflated out of all proportion. And the third side of the religious triangle – what is experienced – is either overlooked or regarded with intense suspicion. Institutional religion is readily intolerant, rapidly exclusive.

Paul by now was in a no-win situation. An embarrassment to his hosts and an irritant to the authorities both Jewish and Roman. All too reminiscent of the final days of Jesus. Pushed from the Sanhedrin to the Roman Governor, Felix, Paul was held in custody and heard again by Felix's successor, Porcius Festus. He was heard, too, by Herod Agrippa.

The charges against Paul could not be made to add up to a criminal offence, and yet, giving the man his freedom would have amounted to the provocation of unwelcome, even dangerous, disorder. Over the course of Paul's period in custody, the bone of contention apparently shifted from his attitude towards the Law of Moses to his preaching of the raising of Jesus from the dead – which even the Pharisees considered blasphemous.

So the divorce between Christianity and Judaism moved another step closer with the imprisonment of Paul.

In the midst of all this, Paul's response, as a Roman citizen, was to appeal to the Roman Emperor. This was another embarrassment, really, since he hadn't been charged with an appropriate offence. However, in the end it must have seemed the easiest thing to do. To pack this unorthodox, rabble-rousing Roman Jew off to Rome. Paul's next and possibly final journey was about to begin; and at least if he got to Rome in one piece, he'd be well and truly on someone else's patch.

*

We spread out two large sheets of Ordnance Survey maps on the dining room table and, with a ruler, drew a pencil line between Turweston Airfield and Oxford Airport. Several heads bent forward to see if this straight line of flight would coincide with any roads on the ground. The problem was that the route most people would take between the two points utilised the A34 – a busy dual carriageway that was neither direct (as Charlie's flight would have been) nor remotely pleasant to run.

At first the network of minor roads that criss-crossed back and forth over our pencilled line seemed to indicate only short stretches of south-bound roadway that finally petered out altogether in the flood plain of the River Cherwell and the Oxford Canal. But as we pulled up our chairs and examined the maps more carefully, a possible route began to emerge. Having bagged a seat at the south end I was best placed to trace the detail.

Starting from crossroads at the edge of Turweston Airfield there was a fairly straight north-south route with narrow lanes and minor roads running through open countryside between tiny villages and hamlets as far as the more substantial village of Middleton Stoney. From there, a slightly busier cross-country road ran directly to Kirtlington – another substantial village with pretty houses and a good pub. But the route across the flood plain posed a headache. There was a circuitous and rather unpleasant but secure, main road, or there was a direct network of footpaths across the plain – boggy at the best of times but in heavy weather, virtually impassable – and Charlie was planning to go in February. No matter. We'd have to get out there and investigate; at least he had the makings of a runnable route – just as well, as sponsorships were already beginning to come in.

In the weeks that followed, Charlie applied himself seriously to fund-raising and began preliminary training in the shape of gentle runs along the Thames tow-path. The rest of the family took on support roles, reporting back to Charlie who was definitely leading from the front.

My elderly mother and I made it our job to firm up the route by car and on foot and, while we were at it, we stopped at all the country pubs along the way, seeking their goodwill and practical help. We ate a lot of lunches and my Mum was enthusiastically persuasive. The landlords were brilliant. Peter appointed himself liaison-person with the police and the airfields, while Sarah and Tim informed Charlie in no uncertain terms that he would not be running alone! The project was taking shape.

*

The story of Paul's sea voyage as a captive to Rome (*in Acts 27:1-44, 28:1-15*) is a glorious piece of writing. So pacey and so visual it brings to mind the wonderful children's picture books available nowadays with simple, almost poetic text imposed on fabulous, full-page illustrations. I don't mean to imply that the voyage described by Luke is just a children's tale – although, having said that, like the most durable of children's stories, it is only superficially simple.

It's an amazing fusion of wondrous journey (where Paul's faith, trust and authority bring miracles and a safe haven) and factual information almost journalistic in its forceful brevity. The terrors described are vivid and the detail casually included about shipping routes and nautical practices lend a hard-edged credibility to the storm sequences. Reading it, I feel that the Luke who wrote it *must* have been Paul's companion of the 'we' passages, or at the very least, someone who took the story straight from his lips.

It's not hard for me to conjure up the first page in this imaginary picture book. The image shows Paul aboard ship, in chains. With him is his guard, a centurion named Julius, a companion named Aristarchus, and Luke himself. The day is gloriously sunny and the sea is blue. Cargo is stowed, anchors are weighed and the vessel is leaving harbour on the first leg of the voyage. A small map, inset at the bottom right hand corner, shows the route from the ship's starting point at Caesarea, hugging the coast as far as Tyre and Sidon, then setting course to sail around the north of Cyprus.

On the next page they're leaving Cyprus behind them and the sails are billowing as they head out towards the port of Myra in Asia Minor. On deck, Paul and his two friends are sitting in the sunshine, deep in conversation, while the centurion maybe chats to the ship's captain.

Turn over, and we have the first intimation of trouble ahead. We're at the docks in Myra, where Paul and company have disembarked only to discover that for the time being, there are no vessels bound for Italy. The port is quiet and run-down, the weather is grey and the men are more warmly dressed than before. For summer is turning to autumn and soon the season of storms will be upon them, obliging ships to postpone long voyages, sticking instead to inshore waters for short journeys during windows of calm.

The following picture introduces a 'baddie' – the impecunious Captain of a battered-looking ship who is willing to risk a late-season voyage in the hope of making a handsome profit on the cargo. He is admitting to Julius, the centurion, that they may indeed be forced to over-winter somewhere along the route but he is clear he is not making any firm plans. He'll go as far as he possibly can.

Paul and the others are merely human cargo; they have no part in the decision. The centurion weighs up the situation. The Captain may talk with a loud voice but he seems at best, unprepared and at worst, foolhardy. On the other hand, this is probably their last chance to leave Myra ... and Julius, wishing to keep going, takes the passage.

*

Questionable decisions. We all make them, particularly when we're desperate to achieve a goal or to rescue a project in which we've over-invested our time or money or emotions. It would have been wiser for Julius to have stayed in Myra. It may have been wiser for Paul to have rescinded his demand to take his case to Rome. And was the Jesus movement itself, wise in allowing Paul to preach its message to all those urban-based, Gentile worshipers of the Greek pantheon, a world away from the hills and villages and the lakeside of Jesus' rural Galilee – and a far cry too from the solemn complexities of Jewish Jerusalem?

But that's miracles. They come without a set of instructions. What is done to encourage and direct a startling new beginning is left up to ordinary, fallible people like you and me, working thoughtfully from our own strengths – but all too often, distorting things through our own weakness. And what is done, is done.

We know now that the decisions of the early church set against the politics of the day, led inexorably to the acrimonious splitting of Christians from their Judaic brethren. Is that what Jesus himself would have foreseen? The acrimony especially seems immeasurably sad to me.

*

Christmas was muggy and wet. January was wet too and in low-lying areas there were floods. Charlie was interviewed by local TV who showed him squelching through muddy fields, training for 4th February. Fund-raising was going well and our spirits were high when Charlie brought a corporate sponsor on board who pledged a substantial sum, should he complete the run, and we began to believe we really could raise a sum that would make a difference. The hospital's own fund-raising team pulled strings too, and gave lots of advice and support. But mostly it was individuals, people who heard Charlie's story and were moved to contribute whatever they could. Away with cynicism, people are amazing!

*

Turn to the next page of Paul's journey and the seedy little cargo ship has set sail, but already things are not going well. The seas are rough and the skies are dark. The Captain is promising a worried-looking Julius that he'll put in to the port of Cnidus until the winds die down. However, though he's unwilling right now to risk the open sea passage to the lee of Crete, he's still planning to go for it.

The following picture shows the ship in harbour, with the crew lashing everything securely to the decks and fresh provisions being carried aboard to see the ship's company through the next stage of the voyage. The inset map shows the route they follow, and the discomfort they suffer is emphasised by a tiny picture of the storm-tossed vessel, with even tinier sea-sick people hanging over the side.

And here, on the next page, they have reached the port of Fair Haven on the southern coast of Crete. The ship is bedraggled but still sea-worthy and this would be a good, sheltered spot to sit tight, make repairs and wait out the winter. A ray of pale sunshine penetrates the clouds as the company, assembled on deck, makes its opinions known to the ship's Captain. A few hardy souls, desperate or greedy, want to press on but the majority believe they've been lucky to get this far. Reasoning they cannot now make it all the way to Italy, they argue to remain in Fair Haven until the spring.

The Captain, however, is on the side of the rash few and it's his decision to make. In a last-ditch attempt to persuade him to act sensibly, Paul – the lowest of the low on this ship – speaks up. He has had a premonition that if they attempt to go further, they'll be caught again and this time their luck will not hold. The ship will go down. His declaration is sombre and there is a silence. But what does Paul know? Is he a mariner? The Captain consults with his supporters. Then he announces there is still time to hug the coast of Crete all the way round to its northern shore, and *there* they will wait for the spring.

Turn over the page and the ship is once more at sea. It's a clear, cool day, the sun is shining from a blue sky and the sailors are laughing merrily as they finally make good headway after weeks of setbacks. Even the passengers seem relaxed. Paul alone is not smiling.

Turn over the page and suddenly the sky is dark with thunder clouds. Everyone is anxious. Only Paul looks calm now, and untroubled.

Then the storm hits. Lightning forks the sky and the rain lashes down as a north-easter sweeps the ship past the western tip of Crete, into the open sea. In a vain attempt to turn the vessel across the wind and back towards land the crew is throwing cargo and even ship's gear overboard to lighten the load. Other sailors are straining on ropes and the Captain is yelling orders that the wind is simply carrying away.

The next page, a double spread, gives a panoramic view in which the doomed vessel is being blown helplessly before the wind, right across the Mediterranean Sea.

And when we turn the page, the inset map shows how the

tempest has tossed the ship, mile after mile, until now it approaches the rocky coast of the island of Malta.

On board, confusion reigns. It is dark but we can make out a number of sailors preparing to launch a small boat, thinking to try and save themselves. Seeing this, Julius has drawn his sword to cut its ropes and set it adrift: the crew and passengers will stay together, whatever their fate. Fear is etched on every face – but Paul's.

And now, in the next illustration, Paul takes charge. He tells the exhausted passengers and crew that they should eat, to prepare themselves for what lies ahead. So the sailors drop their storm anchors and while the ship is washed more slowly but relentlessly towards land, Paul prays, breaks bread and distributes it. The sea foams, the deck tilts but on board there are a few precious moments of calm as Paul tells everyone to pluck up their courage and no lives need be lost.

Next picture, it's daybreak. Jagged rocks guard a sandy cove towards which they are moving. Quickly the sailors pull up the storm anchors and untie the ship's steering paddle. They will try to beach the ship on the sandy bottom as near to shore as they can … already, some swimmers are jumping into the water, while others grab planks to keep themselves afloat. On the shore, running towards the beach are two or three people. They have seen the shipwreck and they're getting ready to rescue survivors – and, of course, to lay their hands on whatever cargo can be brought ashore.

Text on the next page reads simply: *Everybody came safely to land; not a single person was lost.* And we see people hugging each other and many surrounding Paul to thank him, while local folk light a huge, warm bonfire on the beach. The Captain sits with a couple of others apart from the rest, pale, dishevelled and bruised. The inset map has a small caption too: *The place where they landed was called Malta.*

In the next picture we see some islanders looking after the

company who are warming themselves by the fire, plus some other islanders who are forming a chain to get anything they can of value off the wreck. But the air of relief and celebration has suddenly been interrupted.

We see a poisonous viper which has jumped from the burning brushwood of the fire and has sunk its fangs into Paul's arm. The Maltese onlookers are horrified, muttering that Paul – who is obviously under guard – must be a murderer, doomed to die. He should have perished in the storm, but having survived he will now be struck down by the snake, according to his fate. The thing is, though, Paul himself looks quite unconcerned and we're told he simply shakes the creature off and carries on as before. The onlookers watch and wait … and to their astonishment, Paul's arm does not swell, he does not writhe in agony – in fact, nothing happens at all. They stare and stare. Is he a god?

Turn over, and Paul and his companions have been taken to lodge with none other than the island's Governor, Publius. Comfortable quarters, indeed, but Paul repays the generous official when his father falls ill with dysentery and Paul is able to lay hands upon him and bring about a cure.

And so, to Rome. In the next picture it is spring and Paul's little group is embarking on a new ship, the 'Castor and Pollux' from Alexandria, bound for Italy. It's a fair day, there's a fair wind and there are smiles all round as, waving farewell, they begin the final leg of their journey.

Just a picture next. The Mediterranean, sparkling and hospitable, and a smart ship in full sail, moving steadily towards the coast of Italy, just visible on the horizon.

Turn over: the city of Rome itself. Paul and the centurion Julius, with Luke and Aristarchus, are on foot while a hired hand leads a donkey, lightly laden with belongings, gathered together over the winter in Malta.

And, look! Coming towards Paul with arms outstretched is a band of Christians. News travels fast, and hearing this famous man was on his way, they've come out to meet him and give thanks for his safe arrival in their city, the capital of the Empire. Never was there such a warm and happy welcome for a captive on his way to prison.

And now, the last picture of all: Paul, citizen of Rome, in prison. Actually, it doesn't look too bad. Spartan, of course, and Paul has an armed guard. But he also has parchment, pen and ink – and visitors. We leave him, talking animatedly to a small, attentive audience and a shaft of sunlight streams through a tiny window high in the wall.

*

Easter is almost upon us, but today I'm grumbling. It's Wednesday in Passion Week and for the third year in succession I can't go to the solemn liturgical singing of the St John Passion in the cathedral, which for me, marks the start of Easter. It's not my fault; I can't go and there's nothing I can do about it ... except grumble.

Furthermore, it's evident that winter, on its way out, has just turned around for a final bite before departing. Suddenly it's bleak and cold and cloudy again, and that's all wrong! Easter should be green shoots and spring lambs, warm air to breathe and a little sunshine so we can leave our coats at home. It isn't just middle-aged me who's fed up, but my children too.. Young, hard-working adults, they're longing to relax out of doors at weekends and they're dreaming of summer, of al fresco meals and holidays. Yet here we are, gearing up for a well-earned break, and Easter is going to be chilly. Lord, why can't we have some sunshine!

I'm slightly shocked by the force of my frustration at something as trivial as inclement weather. I sit down with a coffee and comfort myself with the thought that, after all, I stand in a long tradition of moaners.

Isn't it the case that, in the marvellous story of the Exodus, the children of Israel were delivered from the Egyptians and guided through the wilderness by a pillar of cloud by day and a pillar of fire by night, and nevertheless they still managed to moan the whole time? Their God was a mighty God, full of signs and wonders – the smiting of enemies, the parting of seas, manna from the skies, water from the rocks – and yet, wonders were never enough; they kept on complaining.

It's interesting, isn't it? Part of us thinks we'd like an interventionist God – the petitionary prayer flows easily, however we rationalise it. But would we really? Even for the best, most elevated purposes? I don't think so. Like developing teenagers who detest even the benign oversight of their worldly-wise parents, we would hate the reality of a busy-body God.

Those Old Testament stories had it absolutely right when they portrayed the patriarchs and the prophets as reluctant, questioning and even angry at their God. The more he intervened, the less they liked it. Whether you prefer to read these stories as history or myth, or something of both, they capture our predicament incredibly astutely.

Most of us, at times, would like our God to be more knowable. We think it might be nice if God would clearly communicate with us now and again – speak to us, even. But then, those Old Testament writers were spot on, for when they told a tale of God actually speaking, the recipients of the message were pretty much universally appalled, reluctant, frightened and not unusually, deaf as posts.

Those brilliant tellers of spiritual tales, with their perceptive evocations of human desire and divine compassion knew that, in truth, mankind needs space and freedom to grow in stature and take responsibility for the way in which human life is played out.

And I know that even if it were no trouble at all for my God to provide for me a gloriously sunny, cheerful Easter week, I'd probably say "No, thanks." How contrary is that?

The thing is, when I stop moaning, I know that life itself is miraculous. There is mystery in all things and beauty to be found even in the raw cold and the cloudy sky and the stark, leafless skeletons of the trees I want so much to burst into green life. No, I wouldn't welcome a higher power that could give me even the best of what I desired, let alone upbeat weather for the convivial consumption of Easter roast lamb and chocolate eggs.

*

Having finally got Paul to Rome, Luke proceeds to inform us, in two short verses *(Acts 28:30-31)* that he remained there for two years, welcoming all who came to see him and proclaiming the message of Jesus Christ *'quite openly and without hindrance'*.

And with that, the double volume, Gospel and Acts, ends.

Hello? Is that it? Is that how it was meant to finish, so abruptly, so – inconclusively? Infuriating, not to know some things. I mean, scholars seem fairly sure that Paul continued to teach and preach for an appreciable time after he reached Rome.

Early church tradition has it that both Peter and Paul were executed during the first major persecution of Christians by the Emperor Nero. Paul's letters to his fledgling churches seem to point to a development in his theological ideas that is not evident in Luke's *Acts*.

So, did Luke lose touch with Paul? Did he not know what became of him? Or was the fate of Paul so well known to Christians like Theophilus, for whom he wrote, that retelling it was unimportant? We'll never know but, for myself, I can't help thinking that Luke did write, or intend to write, more – another chapter, another book even, but perhaps he was not spared for long enough to accomplish the task.

Whatever the reason, Luke ends his work with the arrival of Paul, Apostle to the Gentiles, in the capital city of the Roman Empire. From here, we know that Christians grew in number and we can chart how their ideas about Jesus of Nazareth became increasingly settled, and how in the course of many centuries, Christianity spread geographically far and wide. Food for much thought for another day.

In the meantime, it is *Acts* that gives us a precious bridge of understanding between the inspirational mission of Jesus in Galilee and Judea and its continuation in the aftermath of his execution in Jerusalem.

And its helter-skelter urgency rings true for me. In *Acts*, signs and wonders jostle with faction-fights and harsh words, healing and enlightenment rub shoulders with curses and cruelty, drama and excitement ,with quiet reflection, and all of it is grounded in time and place: the named people, the actual towns, the mappable journeys.

To me it speaks clearly of the energy unleashed by the joy of a miracle, and the triumphs and disasters that ensued as fallible humans struggled to give it substance and direction. It's a wonderful book.

Furthermore, for me, *Acts* has become a text that has helped to address my question of what happens to people *after* a miracle. The answer? Confusion, joy, the need to work, the inevitability of grief, the struggle to attain a new balance, the need to accept others' gifts, then growth if you're lucky, and eventually some clarity.

That's what I think happens – amidst all the wrong turnings and dead ends, the disasters and the triumphs. And it's all there in *Acts*.

*

When I placed the full stop after the words: ... *'like no other.'* ... I knew for sure I'd reached the end of my scruffy diary. In truth, it being five years since Charlie's accident, the diary had almost petered out, with entries now few and far between. So, when I picked up my pen a day or two after his run, I was acutely conscious that I was rounding off the record to close the little book, and, writing fast, I found myself having to hold back unexpectedly mixed and powerful emotions.

The day dawns. 4th February, sunny and crisp. Charlie and co are up uncomfortably early but in good spirits. Only one query hangs over the route and that is whether the direct cross-country end-stage across the flood-plain of the Cherwell is actually passable. As luck would have it, yesterday, despite the rain stopping, the swollen river burst its banks, cutting off footpath access to the bridge the runners will have to cross. The whole area was spectacularly flooded and it seems pretty unlikely to have cleared by today. But refusing to accept defeat as certain, I leave them to their breakfast, and with my heart in my mouth I take the car to do a recce. I'm hoping against hope the team will be able to stick to the 3 mile direct finish. A detour will add two extra, dreary, traffic-plagued miles of main road, right near the end when stamina will be low. I park the car by a muddy farmyard and tread the footpath towards the river. Holding my breath …

It's extraordinary! The water level has gone down overnight and though it still looks like a marsh, the path is just about distinguishable: a narrow ribbon of firmer ground, winding its way to the bridge. I know this is how a flood-plain works - but I couldn't have a more graphic demonstration of the folly of building houses on such useful land. OK the runners will need to be guided for a quarter of a mile or so, since they don't know where to look for the path – but though it isn't immediately obvious, it is soggily, muddily there. Sorted.

The day properly begins at Turweston Airfield, near the control tower, at the actual site of the crash. A solemn moment. Only a few officials are around this early but a collecting jar in the café is full and messages of support are picked up.

Then, to the car park of the pub at the southern edge of the airfield. Here the run is to begin and we meet up with a journalist and a photographer from the local paper, and, right on time, a police motor-cyclist joins us to act as escort for the runners. Oh my! Suddenly the project is excitingly, scarily 'official'.

Obediently, the runners line up for a photo: Charlie is to the fore with brother Tim and friend Rob (the only one with experience of pacing a marathon). An army cousin who can be relied upon to be super-fit completes the quartet who'll run the whole way but three others line up as well. Sarah is going to join her brothers at the half-way point and is bringing her generous, supportive boyfriend to run too, while Peter's sister, rashly deciding that the middle-aged stratum of the family should be represented, is intent on running the final six miles.

The car-park also contains a support team, shivering in the frosty morning. There's Peter, of course, and me, each of us with a car laden with drinks to set up at strategic points along the way.

Peter's parents accompany him and my mother comes with me. Melissa arrives with a car to do extra jobs and trouble-shooting as necessary, while the finish line at Oxford Airport is manned – womanned? – by my sister and Tim's wife (who, to his great good fortune married him the year before) aided by some enthusiastic members of staff from the airport's Leisure Centre.

Back at the start, there are interviews, pictures, warm-ups and finally ... the police bike pulls away and the runners are off! In no time they round the first corner and are out of sight. For a second, those of us left behind look at one another in astonishment before, galvanised into action, we pile into our cars.
Mum and I head for the first drinks station, a pub forecourt in a little

village five and a half miles away. I drive with care, as some of the shaded sections of road are still icy and once or twice we skid slightly. We'll have to overtake the runners at some stage and, rounding every bend, we scan the way ahead for them – until I begin to feel uneasy.

I'd written out detailed route instructions – over-detailed really – but the first bit of the route was confusingly criss-crossed with tiny lanes and farm tracks and I start to suspect they've taken a wrong turning … Then, relief … there they are, up ahead, having covered a lot of ground already… but are they going too fast? I hope not.

We ease past them with a toot of the horn and drive on to set up the first of five drinks stations – all of them outside pubs, most of whom are collecting money for us as well.

Mum and I assemble our small table and put out water while Melissa turns up and is first to hear the police bike and spot the runners coming into view. Loud cheers as the four lads smile and wave and smoothly collect their drinks, for all the world like elite marathon types. And once again, in no time, they're through the village and out of sight.

Mum and I clear up and overtake the runners a couple of miles further on, noting with satisfaction they're still going well, before we head towards the half-way point at Middleton Stoney. We arrive to find that Peter has not only set up his table but has also organised coffee all round for the supporters. What a star!

We watch Sarah and boyfriend warm up, ready to augment the small band of runners. And here they are! The policeman by now is thoroughly in the spirit of the occasion and, beaming, leads his little team slowly past the drinks table. The two additions are greeted with delight as they fall in with the pace and the company – now of six – go on their way.

They set off for five miles of long straight road through woodland – attractive but a slog. However, adding runners turns out, providentially, to be a brilliant move. They inject new excitement and keep up the steady pace.

At Kirtlington, the next stage on the route, we're joined by Charlie's godparents. 'Our' pub has just opened and they chat merrily to customers, explaining what's going on. Meanwhile, Peter's sister limbers up and her husband arrives to lend a hand at the drinks station. The sun, so pale earlier, is now shining brightly and onlookers gather, many of them donating cash to the cause. A carnival atmosphere prevails as the runners come into view.

Peter's sister pulls a face, takes a deep breath and runs in alongside the others. Now they're seven. It's noticeable that Charlie is concentrating fiercely and they're keeping to a very respectable time, though it's surely getting to be hard work for him. Once again, though, the addition of another runner lifts the spirits. Quite an athlete in her youth, Peter's sister has lost neither her technique nor her determination and she contributes a dose of valuable strength and confidence.

Only a couple of miles further on we set up the next drinks station - at the start of the cross-country stretch across rutted fields and down a steep hill to the flood plain below. We're hoping the change from road running and the stunning scenery will give them a psychological boost - although it's bound to slow them down a bit. We're only just ready when the runners approach, moving as one, in tight formation, and it's clear that Charlie's gait, not completely even at the best of times, is distinctly lop-sided now. His not-quite-straight right foot tends to have of a mind of its own and he looks as if he's tiring and, yes, hurting. The cross-country section will bring them near to the finish but the going will be rough and once they reach the plain, it'll also be heavy.

While the main body of the support team makes its way to the final drinks station at a pub beside the Oxford Canal, Mum and I drive to the hamlet where the runners' footpath meets the plain. Leaving Mum in the car, I squelch my way across a field and position myself to guide the group to the bridge across the River Cherwell. I wait. And wait. Doubts begin to trouble my mind. Was it foolish to go for the footpaths? Has the demanding terrain been too much for Charlie's leg? And I'm just convincing myself that disaster has struck when I spot them in the distance and wave frantically. The lead runner waves back. They come closer, running very slowly, bunching tightly around Charlie, and I set off in front of them, slipping and sliding along the muddy path, cursing my arthritic lack of agility. Even Charlie is moving faster than me, and by the time I reach the bridge, they're close on my heels. With relief I stand aside and, one by one, they slither across the wooden footbridge to regain the path as it heads up through scrubland on the other side. They'll soon be at the last drinks station and a crowd of well-wishers will, hopefully, speed them on.

Not me though. I have to plough my way back again through the mud to the car, and I dearly want to be able to cheer my brave son – well, all of them - on to the finish line. I think that, somehow, they'll get Charlie through and I really, really want to be there. But as my boots sink into the boggy ground I gloomily admit to myself I could miss the last act. And then, quite suddenly, out of nowhere a farmer appears in a Land Rover. With immense gratitude I accept a lift back to the car, where my mother is patiently waiting, clutching a high-denomination note that's been pressed into her hand by the farmer's wife. How kind everyone has been!

Between the canal and the airport there's a stretch of main road and to our joy we see the group moving slowly and doggedly ahead. Our police motor-cyclist has picked them up again and is leading them homeward. Mum and I overtake. Charlie is somewhere in the middle of the bunch, running unsteadily but rhythmically in step with the others. And stride by painful stride he's getting closer to his goal.

I swing the car into the Leisure Centre car park at Oxford Airport and Mum and I hastily join a surprisingly large and expectant crowd. Amongst them, local TV is already filming and I'm thrilled to see that Martin McNally, Charlie's Consultant from the Limb Reconstruction

Unit, has made it to greet him. A tape has been stretched across the road. As the runners turn into the airport complex, we jump and wave and cheer. The police bike peels off, Charlie's six support runners fall back and Charlie, finding strength from goodness knows where, runs on to break the tape.

And suddenly everyone is hugging one another. Charlie falls into Melissa's arms. Peter and I embrace and I'm laughing and crying at the same time. A few moments for a very shaky Charlie to recover somewhat and then the TV cameras record Martin McNally heartily congratulating him. Some swift mental arithmetic confirms that a truly substantial sum of money has been raised. The Leisure Centre puts on hot drinks, and Charlie, with interviews still to do, rests his aching, shaking, weary body under Melissa's protective gaze.

For me, the rest of the day is a haze. I have never been so proud. Not just proud of Charlie but of everyone. The whole family, close friends and amazingly generous folk who didn't know us at all - but helped and contributed to the fund and made the day utterly special. The magic carried on into the evening as family and friends ate and drank together and laughed and relaxed and forgot the time, as you do: a celebration like no other.

* * *

CLARITY

When I started this Lenten project I never really thought I'd learn anything profound. I knew that revisiting Charlie's miracle would be difficult at times but fascinating and (if I could keep it up) it would be full of small, unexpected insights. But, I thought that, nearing the end, I'd have to consider very carefully what, if anything, I'd seriously gained from the exercise. And as for developing my practice of *Lectio Divina*, I knew from the outset I was still a beginner.

But here I am; the week after Easter. I've read *Acts* right through (plus a swift study of any and every book I came across that seemed to promise a better understanding of it) and somewhat to my surprise, the enterprise has quite decisively come together. Well, I expect any experienced practitioner of *Lectio* would be wringing their hands in despair at my undisciplined wanderings, but, yes, I have learnt a lot - such a lot - that's definite, interesting and, for me, profound.

To begin with Charlie's story. The 'whole picture', by which I mean not only his small miracle but also its aftermath, has become entire in my mind, whereas before, it consisted of disparate chunks of memory, some sharp from frequent retelling and others – particularly the troubling bits, fading fast.

Memory was interesting. Not just *what* I remembered but the *kinds* of things. As you'd expect, most of my memories were focused on particular events but there were entries, too, that brought to mind pervasive and difficult moods: the struggle to keep cheerful during the 'long hot summer of the wheelchair' for instance.

And I have to admit that going through the scruffy diary corrected some of the 'false memories' I'd accumulated along the way. For example, my recollection of the order of events and the time span between them, was occasionally quite wrong. And maybe this later project is factually no better. For psychologists warn us that any revisiting of the past inevitably instigates additional 'false memories' as we retell stories to ourselves in ever more coherent forms. I'm sure that's true, but a bald statement of facts with no interpretation at all is about as much use to us as an elegant-looking theorem with no explanation of what it's *for*. And the clarity I think I now possess is not really to do with facts but with *meaning*.

I needed to recount the whole of Charlie's story in order to seek out the process by which we as a family re-started our lives after a joyful but shattering life experience. And I guess that was the question with which I began: "How do people ever manage to return to 'normal' after a miracle?"

The answer I've taken so long to discover, is that despite there being a process by which people like us can and do return to everyday life, 'normal' may no longer be our goal.

Jairus' daughter's mother could, I think, in time have returned to the market place to haggle over the price of fish with the best of them – and maybe she did. But speaking for myself, I think I've consumed much too much time and energy over the years, trying to recover a state that I no longer really desire. This, as a piece of learning, came to me as the wholly unexpected result of reading the scruffy diary in tandem with my Lenten slow-reading of *Acts*. I'll try and explain.

Looking back on the miracle that was Charlie's survival and his fight to regain fitness, I'm struck by the fullness of my life then, and by the evidence of my (and my family's) heightened sense of 'awareness' during that whole, roller-coaster period: my openness to joy and to tears and the frequency with which emotional exhaustion forced me to take refuge in solitude. I remember weeping bitterly at the plight of war victims in the news and sometimes having to turn the television off, being unable to take any more of it. I remember the incredible happiness of the day Charlie's Ilizeroff frame was finally removed ... and the terrible disappointment of the moment when the light post-operative bandaging was removed to reveal a thin, wasted shin that looked so fragile it would snap if he so much as sneezed. I remember feeling hugely vulnerable to other people's aggression, so that even their slight annoyance left me puzzled and hurt. I remember thinking over and over: "I can't live like this; I have to rebuild my defences."

And so I tried, and to quite a large extent I was successful. Before long I could watch the news and not flinch at footage of starving children or piles of human corpses or the smoke and flame of bombs. Before long, I could stop my heart from skipping a beat if someone raised their voice at me over a misunderstanding. Before long, I felt my mind was well on the way to regaining its customary supremacy over my emotions.

But soon, I was also beginning not to notice the spring, not to feel privileged and lucky, and not to impulsively reach out to others who I knew who were worried or sad.

I was learning again how my energies could be managed, my compassion prioritised, and my sensitivity to sorrow, protected. But if you ask me now to recall the greatest moments of pride and joy in my life to date, many, many of them will be clustered into that short period when Charlie's future was uncertain and I had no defences to speak of at all. When I relied heavily on the love of my family and the encouragement of friends and when I appreciated every small good thing that came my way.

By the beginning of Lent this year, when I started all this, I was almost back into my metaphorical suit of defensive armour, the shell that had fallen off when Charlie's aeroplane crashed. And I was sure that it wasn't possible to function without such emotional protection. Now I believe I was wrong. Of course it isn't *easy* to live in an open, undefended way and hardly anyone actually manages to come close, but this is what I think St Paul's expression 'living in Christ' means in practice.

For the Jesus of the gospels was utterly open, both to the divine and to the joys and sorrows of men and women. He wept, he partied, he took trouble to pitch his teachings so that his disciples could understand, he was respectful and kind towards sinners and outcasts and children. And in *Acts* we get a glimpse of how those who knew Jesus, and those who knew *them* in turn, took on this extraordinary quality of openness in so far as they were able.

My early Christian 'companions', Peter and Paul, John, James, Stephen, Barnabus, John Mark, Timothy and the others, were far from perfect people but they lived – passionately, committedly and with love – for others. And although they certainly did a lot of soul-searching (being open doesn't, I think, mean a forgetting or a neglect of self) they were always turned *outwards* towards those who wanted and needed the spiritual insights they could offer. From *Acts* I clearly see that to live as a Christian is, above all, to be caringly *responsive*, whatever the cost. Which doesn't mean they got it right all the time, either. *Acts* is reassuringly replete with harsh words and hasty actions. The early Christians weren't clones of one another. They lived out their callings according to their lights, in the best ways they knew how. It didn't always go smoothly, and I, who am frightened of failure, take great heart from this.

Naïve? Impractical? Doomed? Well, as the movement grew and expanded, worldliness, money and power crept in. Down the ages, one could point to endless instances of abuse and wickedness sanctioned by the Christian churches. But the astonishing thing is, that for those who really want to understand, the message contained in the gospels and *Acts* concerning the teachings and actions and relevance of Jesus of Nazareth is as strong and simple and accessible – and difficult as ever it was. And when we look at the lives of 'good' people, both biblical and contemporary, we find that the quality they have in common is openness, and the behaviour we admire stems from compassion.

I doubt I shall ever be able to dismantle all my defences and return to that intensity of experience that was my life in the weeks and months of Charlie's miracle. But I'm going to stop right now trying to build them up any further, and who knows, maybe I shall find the courage to discard what I have, little by little, so that I can once again find laughter and tears and suffering and delight in the experiences not just of my own life but of all the lives that touch mine.

I'm under no illusion, however; that to move in this direction will require *courage*: the courage to feel deeply and act boldly; the courage to love unconditionally and delight in simple things. So much hot air, you think? Vague aspirations like 'apple pie and motherhood' that are beyond criticism? But the awfulness is, I … we … don't really crave such awesome things. We're afraid to feel deeply, too safety-conscious to act boldly, too mean to love unconditionally, and too sophisticated to delight in simple things. It is not a recipe for constant happiness or a route to the top rung of the social ladder, but it is a way, *the way*, I think, to live life to the full. Hard and costly though it may be at times, if we can resist the temptation to protect ourselves from other people's hurt and damage, we can open ourselves, too, to all the wonders that life offers.

Theologically, I think that to 'live in Christ' must be to experience, here and now, the Kingdom of Heaven that Jesus talked about so often. No, of course we inattentive, unremarkable individuals can only catch hold of it fleetingly, but if something – a small miracle, say – comes our way, perhaps we may grasp, experience and remember what real life means.

*

I'm astonished to have reached the end. And absurdly reluctant to let go. I look out of the window and then get up to make myself a cup of tea. There's a lot of tea and coffee in these reflections. Waiting for the kettle to boil, I phone Charlie on the pretext of asking him about his young son's birthday. Actually, I just want to hear his voice. It's lunchtime but he answers his mobile at his desk. He's cheerful and pleased to talk for a moment but I can tell he's busy. He's past thirty now and work consumes much of his time and attention, as I guess it must for the time being. But he's happy to lay it aside for while and chat about his home and his family. He knows what he's working *for*, his priorities are sound and this I'm sure is a legacy of his brush with premature death. Otherwise, he's much like any other young man, and he's busy and somewhat preoccupied with work this lunchtime. So I sigh with maternal resignation and allow him to get on with it.

Back at my desk I gaze into my computer's mesmerising screen-saver. I must finish. I click back into the text and it occurs to me that in a few short weeks this project has become a compulsive habit, even something of a consolation – how extraordinary.

But I won't have it! I don't need to be consoled. All I need to do now is to press on with the miracle of life and living – nothing more to be said.

* * *

BOOKS

O is a symbol of the world, of oneness and unity. In different cultures it also means the "eye", symbolizing knowledge and insight. We aim to publish books that are accessible, constructive and that challenge accepted opinion, both that of academia and the "moral majority".

Our books are available in all good English language bookstores worldwide. If you don't see the book on the shelves ask the bookstore to order it for you, quoting the ISBN number and title. Alternatively you can order online (all major online retail sites carry our titles) or contact the distributor in the relevant country, listed on the copyright page.

See our website www.o-books.net for a full list of over 400 titles, growing by 100 a year.

And tune in to myspiritradio.com for our book review radio show, hosted by June-Elleni Laine, where you can listen to the authors discussing their books.

mySpiritRadio